YATES COUNTY CHRONICLES

STORIES *from* PENN YAN, KEUKA LAKE AND THE HEART OF THE FINGER LAKES

RICHARD S. MACALPINE

THE History PRESS

Published by The History Press
Charleston, SC 29403
www.historypress.net

The majority of photos come from the collection of the Yates County History Center (YCHC) in Penn Yan, New York. Uncredited photos belong to the author.

Front cover, top: Scene along the shores of Keuka Lake, circa 1890. *Courtesy of YCHC*; *bottom*: Postcard of Main Street in Penn Yan. *Courtesy of YCHC*.
Back cover, top: Author's house on Keuka Lake, circa 1910. *Courtesy of YCHC*.

First published 2014

Manufactured in the United States

ISBN 978.1.62619.329.1

Library of Congress CIP data applied for.

CONTENTS

Acknowledgements 5
Introduction 7

PART I: 1850 to 1900
1. Yates County's Women's Rights Convention (1855) 13
2. Conflagration: The Great Penn Yan Fire of 1872 17
3. The Penn Yan Mystery: Leon Lewis 25
4. Leon Lewis Revisited: Another Penn Yan Mystery 34
5. Penn Yan's Whale Tale 41
6. The Strange Case of County Treasurer James Burns 45
7. Keuka Lake's Steamboat Wars 54
8. Keuka Lake's Biggest Fish Story 59

PART II: 1900 to 1920
9. The Night the Sheppard Opera House Burned 69
10. The Cannon in the Courthouse Park 74
11. *Titanic* Remembered 81
12. Yates County and Women's Suffrage 85
13. Susan Miller Dorsey (1857–1946) 91

PART III: 1920 to 1940
14. Paul Garrett: Yates County's Wine Tycoon 97
15. "Wild Bill" Albertson and His Miller Special 107

16. Tales from "the Pines": French Gold, Ghosts, Hermits, Suburbia and the Klan 111
17. The Penn Yan Cuban Giants and the 1924 Season 119
18. Yates County and the Klan 123
19. FDR and Yates County 131

PART IV: 1940 to 1960
20. The Crash of Milligan's Rats 141
21. Duane Eddy's Yates County Years 144
22. The Last Man at the Benham 149

Notes 155
Bibliography 157
About the Author 159

ACKNOWLEDGEMENTS

By far, the major source for all of the articles that I have written for *Yates Past*, the bimonthly publication of the Yates County History Center (YCHC), are the wonderful resources that are in the Research Center of the Yates County History Center on Chapel Street in Penn Yan. Being the fourth-oldest county historical society in the state of New York (founded in 1860), YCHC has accumulated an amazing collection of files on families who have lived in the county, businesses, places, events, etc. When I get an idea for an article, those files are the first place that I look. Sometimes, it's those files that give me the idea for an article to begin with.

As must be apparent from reading my articles, I rely heavily on the local newspapers. For my view, the greatest resources available at the History Center are the bound editions of the *Yates County Chronicle*, the *Chronicle-Express* and the *Penn Yan Democrat*. (My eyes couldn't handle reading them on microfilm.)

The Yates County History Center has a loyal corps of volunteers and three hardworking paid staff members. I would especially like to point out the contribution to this book made by the curator, Charles R. Mitchell. Chuck ran the Photographic Center on Main Street in Penn Yan for many years, until he could see that digital photography was going to change the business significantly. His experience in that business has made him an effective curator, as there our over ten thousand images in the collection. Many of the images used in this book are part of the History Center's collection. Chuck located these for me and prepared them for publication.

There are two people in the community who have proven invaluable to me in writing several of these articles. One is Yates County Historian Fran Dumas. When I had questions or gaps in my research on a local topic, Fran helped, and I appreciate that. The second is Joan Hand of the Penn Yan Public Library. Joan has a special interest in local history and spends much time on microfilm looking over the old newspapers. What she finds, she prints out and puts in files. Those files are a valuable resource and have given me ideas for articles. For example, her research inspired my articles on Leon Lewis, county treasurer James Burns and the Penn Yan Cuban Giants.

For several of these articles, I relied on the input of people who had firsthand knowledge of the topic. I acknowledged most of them in the articles themselves. I would like to add John Barden and Paul Sprague, who helped me with the article on Paul Garrett. John is in Paul Garrett's family tree and supplied me with useful information and family photos. Paul Sprague is the curator of the Greyton H. Taylor Wine Museum in Hammondsport, New York.

Finally, I would like to thank my loyal corps of proofreaders for every article that I do for *Yates Past*, including the ones in this book. They not only correct obvious mistakes but also offer constructive criticism and ask questions that force me to bring more into focus what I am trying to say. They include my wife, Jeanie; YCHC curator Chuck Mitchell and his wife, Melissa; YCHC director John Potter, YCHC administrative assistant Lisa Harper and her mother, Ruth Hartmann; and YCHC collections assistant Mary Collins. For the five years I have been the editor of *Yates Past*, they have helped me make sure that every issue that goes to the printer is the best quality that it can be.

INTRODUCTION

One thing that I have discovered about myself in retirement is that I have the soul of a researcher. It is one activity that I can get wrapped up in doing and totally lose track of time. I wish I had had just a little bit of that back in my college days, but I didn't. My interest in historical research started to develop during my thirty-four-year career of teaching history at the high school in Oneida, New York. Then I had the interest but not the time. The demands of teaching allowed few opportunities for research during the school year, and summers in the early years were spent taking courses at nearby colleges or painting houses to make ends meet for a growing family.

What sparked my interest in research was an old photograph from my parent's collection. The photo showed my grandfather as a young man standing outside a small grocery store with three other men. The sign above the store read "Cornell & McAlpine." I remember wondering about that photo when I was a kid. I barely remember my grandfather; he died when I was five. All that my mother could say about the photo was that she thought the store was on Market Street in Corning.

In the summer of 1990, I rented a cottage for our family on Keuka Lake. We hit a string of rainy days, and on one of them, I had the thought of going down to the library in Corning to see if I could learn something about my grandfather's grocery store. I guessed at his age in the photo and placed the photo in the very early 1900s. At the library, I looked at Corning city directories starting in 1900. In the 1902 directory, I found the store under "Grocers, 'Cornell & McAlpine'" at 26 Market Street. I asked for the 1902 microfilm roll for the Corning *Evening Leader* and started to read through a column marked "City News." In an April 1902 paper, I found this: "Cornell & McAlpine's grocery is taking on a most inviting appearance and these popular, hustling young men are enjoying a patronage that is good encouragement for their progressiveness." I wondered how long the business lasted because I knew my grandfather moved on to other places. I read every issue until I found the answer in one from April 1903: "The grocery firm of Cornell & McAlpine was dissolved yesterday by Mr. Cornell purchasing the interest of Mr. McAlpine." In those issues that I browsed, I found several somewhat creative, and at times deceptive, advertisements for their business. For example, this one at the time of the national coal strike of 1902 that forced the price of coal up to $6 a ton: Big, bold headline: "Chestnut Coal $3 a Ton!" Small print: "We wish we could sell you coal for $3 a ton, but we can't. We are not even in the coal business, but we ARE in the GROCERY BUSINESS!" And then they went on to list their specials for that week.

As I was looking for more about their business, an unrelated headline caught my eye as I was going through the microfilm: "Four Inch Lizard Found in Harry Lee's Stomach." Under it was a story about a guy who drank water out of a spring on a hot summer day and later became sick with a condition that baffled his doctors. He complained to them about having a sensation in bed at night of something trying to crawl up his throat. Eventually, after three years, he "ejected" the (dead) lizard—what a great story! At any rate I was hooked on this kind of research. I found out all I wanted to know (and more) about my grandfather's grocery store and that old family photo. The information was there. All I had to do was go looking for it. On top of that, I was entertained in the process.

Thus began my research into family history. I started with the federal censuses. I was still teaching in Oneida, New York, at the time, and years before Ancestry.com and the Internet, the nearest place to view the census was on microfilm at the central library in Syracuse. So I would get going early on Saturday mornings and be at the library when it opened. I would grab a microfilm reader and observe the passing of various family members' lives ten years at a time. I discovered that on each branch of my family tree, going back four or five generations, my relatives mostly lived within thirty miles of the shoreline of Keuka Lake.

I wanted much more than just genealogical data, however. I wanted to know what kind of people my ancestors were. I wanted to know what their interests were, what they did for a living, what organizations they belonged to, etc. In 1992, we bought into a small trailer park on Keuka Lake, which

The photo that triggered over twenty-five years of interest in genealogy and local history: Cornell & McAlpine Grocers on Market Street in Corning, New York. My grandfather Ernest McAlpine is on the far right of the photo. *Author's collection.*

gave me a base of operations for research on Saturdays and school vacations. I went to libraries in Dundee, Penn Yan, Naples and Hammondsport and got into the old newspapers on microfilm—the *Dundee Observer*, *Yates County Chronicle*, *Penn Yan Democrat*, *Hammondsport Herald* and the *Naples Record*. After ten years of intense research, visits to courthouses and cemeteries and a few lucky breaks running into distant cousins with important resources, I am reasonably satisfied that I can tell the story of my family from the 1740s to the present.

Along the way, I developed a deep interest and appreciation for local history in the three counties where I had done the bulk of my research: Yates, Steuben and Ontario. When I retired, one of my colleagues asked me what I was going to do with my time. My response was that among other things, I was going to see if I could get involved with the Yates County Genealogical & Historical Society, as it was called at that time. I had spent many hours in their research center in their Oliver House Museum in

Penn Yan doing research and felt comfortable there. After I retired from teaching, we moved into a house on Keuka Lake, just outside Penn Yan, which made that option convenient. My association with the Yates County History Center began with my doing family history research in the early 1990s. After my retirement from teaching in 2001, I became a volunteer working on small projects, was asked to serve on committees and then to serve on the board of directors. I wrote my first article for *Yates Past* in 2004, have written over ninety more since then and have served as its editor since 2008. The Yates County History Center has kept me busy and has given me an opportunity to make a meaningful contribution in retirement. That is why I have dedicated this book to the History Center, and all royalties made from the sale of it will go to the organization in the form of a donation. This book is a collection of some of the articles that I have written.

I am not a native of Yates County; I grew up in New Jersey. My mother, however, was a Penn Yan native and my father grew up in Geneva. As long as I can remember, we would come to this area for summer vacation, spending time on Keuka Lake and in Penn Yan and Geneva. Growing up in the suburban sprawl of the New York metropolitan area, I thought this part of New York State was paradise. I always had the thought that when I retired, I wanted to live here, and now I do.

For a small rural county that was established in 1823, the history of "little Yates" is rich and diverse. While it was mostly rural, it had the thriving villages of Penn Yan, Dundee, Rushville and Dresden, in addition to smaller communities with unique histories. Though staunchly conservative in politics, there was a stubborn streak of reform-minded progressivism. With shorelines on three of the major Finger Lakes (Keuka, Seneca and Canandaigua), geography played a major role in the county's history. Grape farming, for example, produced both a healthy wine industry and an influential temperance movement.

As a researcher and a writer, there is a lot for me to work with here in Yates County. Having taught the broad strokes of American history for so long, I was fascinated to see how the local area was impacted by national trends and world events—immigration, industrialization, technology, wars and depressions. All of that should come across in the variety of articles presented in *Yates County Chronicles*.

RICH MACALPINE
Penn Yan, New York

PART I

1850 TO 1900

1
YATES COUNTY'S WOMEN'S RIGHTS CONVENTION (1855)

There is a building on Main Street in Penn Yan that I have often wondered about. It is on the corner of Main and Court Streets just across from the Yates County Courthouse Park. It is an apartment building today, based on the number of electric meters on the outside. It was a private residence for many years before that, but the architecture isn't that of a private home. It was built to be a church in the early 1850s. The Methodist congregation in Penn Yan split over the issue of slavery, though not because there was a proslavery faction in the church. The issue was how far one should go in opposing slavery. Should a person violate federal law by harboring runaway slaves in his or her home? The more radical faction believed that a "higher law" needed to be obeyed by supporting the Underground Railroad. That faction built the edifice shown in the photo, and it became the Wesleyan Methodist Church. The split in the Methodist congregation lasted until 1864, when the Wesleyan congregation disbanded and the building was sold. It was a private residence well into the twentieth century.

During the Wesleyan Church's residence in the building, a significant women's rights convention was held there. The convention began on January 10, 1855, just seven years after the first women's rights convention was held in Seneca Falls. The local organizers of the event were Mrs. Abner (Alida) Bridgman and Mrs. Stafford C. (Obedience) Cleveland (an ironic name for a feminist leader) of Penn Yan. According to articles in the January 16, 1855 *Yates County Whig*, "A very large and respectable assemblage of

300 Main Street in Penn Yan, New York, was built in 1851 as the Wesleyan Church. *Author's collection.*

men and women were present, a great proportion of whom were from the surrounding towns."

One of the two main speakers at the convention was Susan B. Anthony of Rochester. Miss Anthony, thirty-five years old at the time, had been active in the antislavery and temperance movements. She had been introduced to Elizabeth Cady Stanton on the streets of Seneca Falls in 1851 and quickly became active in the women's rights movement. She addressed the convention in the afternoon session and started her program by asking that a resolution be passed that claimed the right to vote for women, basing her argument on the idea that "taxation without representation is tyranny." The resolution was unanimously adopted. In the main part of her program, Miss Anthony touched on the issues of educational and employment opportunities for women. She told those in attendance, "Woman is the greatest enemy of her own sex! She spurns the betrayed but feels flattered by the attentions of the betrayer!" She closed her part of the program by asking for names on petitions to be sent to the New York legislature demanding the "Elective Franchise." The *Yates County Whig* reported, "Miss Susan B. Anthony of

Rochester addressed the Convention in a speech of considerable length, and much ability and power. She is an excellent speaker and capable of interesting her hearers to an absorbing degree. She was particularly forcible on the remarkable inequality existing between men and women as to the rights of property and the privileges of honorable employment."

The main speaker at the evening session was Ernestine L. Rose of New York City. Considering where American society was in the decade before the Civil War, Mrs. Rose was on the surface quite "out of sync." She was a Polish immigrant and, though born Jewish, was an avowed atheist. Despite all that, she was elected president of the National Women's Rights Convention in 1854 by men and women who were overwhelmingly Protestant and motivated by religious principles. She was called the "Queen of the Platform" and was considered by some to be the best female orator of her time. At the time of her appearance in Penn Yan, she was forty-five years old and had been in the United States for nearly twenty years. Her speech that evening lasted two and a half hours. According to Alida Bridgman, who wrote a summary for the local newspaper: "Mrs. Rose's language is simple, plain, and to the point; and the beauty of her diction is perhaps enhanced by her foreign accent. Her power of enchanting an audience is truly wonderful." In her speech, Rose said:

> *Women's Rights are human rights! It is deemed a final answer to all claim for Women's Rights that St. Paul told the women to submit themselves to their husbands. To this it may be replied that had our forefathers consulted the same authority, our liberties would not have been established, for the taxes and adherence to the British crown had all the advantage of Scriptural authority. Are we not told to render unto Caesar that which is Caesar's and that the powers that be are ordained by God? Had our revolutionary patriots adhered to that authority, Boston Harbor would never have been converted into a magnificent teapot and our liberties would not have been established. Let women follow their example!*

The next time you are driving on Main Street in Penn Yan and are near the courthouse park, look at that building for a minute and think about the fiery orator whose words echoed off its walls in the name of human rights over a century and a half ago. Also, do an Internet search on Ernestine L. Rose. She lived a fascinating life and was a tough, inspirational leader. She was as active in the abolitionist movement as she was in women's rights. Her atheism, her passionate speeches and her radical stand incurred the

Susan B. Anthony, circa 1850. *Wikipedia, public domain.*

wrath of many. Once when she spoke in Maine, a newspaper editor wrote, "It would be shameful to listen to this woman, a thousand times below a prostitute." In South Carolina, a minister forbade his congregation to listen to "this female devil."[1]

In a January 9, 1877 letter to Susan B. Anthony, Rose summed up her career:

> *All I can tell you is that I used my humble powers to the uttermost, and raised my voice in behalf of Human Rights in general, and the elevation and Rights of Women in particular, nearly all my life. Yet in spite of hardships, for it was not easy to travel at that time as now; and the expense, as I never made a charge or took up a collection. I look back to that time, when a stranger and alone, I went from place to place, in highways and byways, did the work and paid my bills with great pleasure and satisfaction; for the Cause gained ground and in spite of the heresies, I had always good audiences, attentive listeners, and was well received wherever I went.*[2]

2

CONFLAGRATION

The Great Penn Yan Fire of 1872

There have been several major fires in the history of downtown Penn Yan. Depending on your age, you may remember the Presbyterian Church going up in flames in 1957, the Main Street Firehouse ten years later or the fire at Pinckney's Hardware in 1985. However, the "granddaddy" of all Penn Yan fires was the one in April 1872 that very well could have wiped out most of the business district if it had not been for the quick action and hard work of local fire departments.

Yates County experienced a prolonged drought through the late winter and spring of 1872. Total snowfall was much lower than that of the average winter, and there was very little spring rain. Farmers complained of conditions in the fields and the level of Keuka Lake was so low that the steamboats weren't able to get to the steamboat landing in the Penn Yan outlet; they had to make their stop at the foot of the lake.

April 30, 1872, was a warm spring day with a strong wind out of the south. The fire started in the late afternoon that day in the foundry of the Commercial Iron Works, which was located across the street from where the Wagner Restaurant is today on East Elm Street (then Jacob Street). The foundry turned out iron beams, plows and threshing machines, among other things. One eyewitness account maintained that sparks would occasionally fly out of the cupola above where the molten iron was poured and set the roof on fire. Workmen would watch for that and go up on the roof with buckets of water to extinguish it. This particular day, the plank leading to the roof broke with the workman on it, which enabled the fire to quickly get out of control.

Visitation of Fire!

Two Hotels, a Foundry, a Carriage Manufactury and Two Business Blocks Burned!

Fifteen Penn Yan Homes in Ashes!

Jacob and Benham Streets Partly Swept!

Canandaigua to the Rescue!

*Headlines from the May 2, 1872 Issue of **Yates County Chronicle***

Headlines from the May 2, 1872 issue of the *Yates County Chronicle*. *Author's collection.*

The photographer is standing with his back to the Four Corners looking down Jacob Street (East Elm today) toward the railroad tracks. The smokestack on the right was where the fire started, the Commercial Iron Works. The house on the left still standing is where the VFW is located today. The main path of the fire was off to the left of the photo (north). *Courtesy of YCHC.*

The fire rapidly enveloped the 1830s-era foundry building, and with the help of the strong south wind, it spread across the street to the Central Hotel and the block of businesses where the Wagner Restaurant and the Sampson Theater are today. It then spread northward on both sides of Benham Street as far as the barn behind the Benham Hotel (site of the Community Bank today). Firemen struggled to save houses on Clinton Street. The fire also spread southward from the foundry to envelop several barns belonging to residences and businesses on Canal Street (Seneca Street today). The wind carried dangerous sparks as far as four miles out of the village into the town of Benton. One house on Head Street (now North Avenue) caught fire as a result. By the time everything was brought under control, forty-one buildings were completely destroyed, including fifteen residences, several barns and henhouses, two hotels (the Central Hotel and the Empire House), two major businesses (the Commercial Iron Works and the Carriage Shop of T. Brigden & Son) and two blocks of small businesses (the Benham Block and the Hicks Block), which housed a music dealer, two grocery shops, a tailor shop, a billiard parlor and bowling alley, a carpenter shop and a blacksmith shop, among other businesses. Total damages were estimated at $130,000, of which insurance covered about half. There was one possible fatality. Thirty-year-old Irish-born Martin Hope, an original member of the Keuka Rifles during the Civil War (Company I of the Thirty-third New York Infantry) was reported missing by his family after the fire, but his remains were never found. According to one account, "There have been several reports as to his untimely end, one being that when the fire alarm was sounded, those persons who were in Kelly's bowling alley ran out into the street, leaving him fast asleep in a back room of the establishment. Another report is that he came out with the rest but went back alone in order to rescue a large Newfoundland dog that was tied in the basement of the block. Certain it is, that after that day he was never again seen."

The devastation from the fire could have been much, much worse. Residents in the area had acted quickly. According to the May 2, 1872 *Yates County Chronicle*:

> *Many took their goods out of their houses and suffered considerable loss, who yet saved their dwellings. There was a prodigious amount of work done by women who, if possible, outdid the men in energy and capacity for effective service. The conditions for a fire were most favorable for its spread and it is only wonderful that it did not extend twice as far as it did in its sweep of devastation. The fire kindled in every fence and cluster of straws, on every roof within its reach, and only vigilance and the utmost watchfulness checked it where it was finally curbed. Our firemen did noble service, aided by the mill, and no doubt succeeded in saving Main Street, for which all should be profoundly grateful.*

Most of the credit for containing the fire went to Penn Yan's fire companies who responded quickly and performed admirably. Keuka No. 1 was credited with saving the businesses along Main Street. The firemen of that company battled the fire using water from the Keuka Lake Outlet and positioning themselves just down Jacob Street with their backs to the Four Corners. Excelsior No. 2 worked to save the Benham House Hotel on Main Street. An eyewitness account reported that men tore down a house on Jacob Street to stop the fire from spreading farther to the east. Carpeting was hung on the house next to that lot and doused with water to defeat the flames.

Again from the *Chronicle*:

> *As soon as the fire began to loom up in its threatening proportions, a telegram was sent to Canandaigua and the gallant firemen of that village responded with astonishing alacrity. In about sixty minutes after the dispatch reached that village, they had sounded the alarm, shipped their Steam Fire Engine and reached Penn Yan by a special train furnished by the Northern Central Railroad. Their running time from Canandaigua to Penn Yan was forty-one minutes. They came with a company of excellent Firemen and the citizens of Penn Yan have reason to be profoundly grateful for their kindness and alacrity in coming so promptly to our rescue in the time of our dreadful peril. The company remained until four o'clock the following morning and the steamer poured a large amount of water over the burned district, extinguishing the fire.*

Another company was summoned from Elmira, but it was intercepted in Watkins and told it was not going to be needed.

Within a month after the fire, rebuilding began, led by Charles Kelly, the owner of the Central Hotel. He rebuilt his hotel—today known as the Universal Building, which houses the Once Again Shop—and it was ready for business by the end of 1872. The Commercial Iron Works constructed a new building on the site of the old one and was back in business in a year. The *Chronicle* in mid-July printed a list of the businesses and houses being rebuilt and stated that "it is worthy of note that most of the new structures are much better buildings than those they replace. No doubt by the end of next year the property destroyed on the 30th of April by the great fire will be nearly all reconstructed and for the most part much better than before."

A few weeks after the fire, this letter appeared in the *Yates County Chronicle*:

> *A Hundred Wise Men—Wednesday morning—the day after the fire—the Oracles and Solons were in fine feather. About a hundred or so of them*

The Benham Block destroyed by the fire. It was located between the Commercial Iron Works and the building at the corner of Main Street that now houses Cam's New York Pizzeria. *Courtesy of YCHC.*

> *knew exactly how the thing should have been managed and they would have engineered matters precisely thus and so and there wouldn't have been any fire, you know. It is very easy to be wise after the event. It was so after every battle in the South; it is so now. If the Oracles would only turn that great stream of breath upon the theme of purchasing immediately a steam fire engine for Penn Yan, that would be to the purpose. Let 'em blow off in that necessary direction and cease not until a No. 1 Silsby is secured which will knock the spots out of a fire in such a manner as to satisfy the most critical and exacting taxpayer.*
>
> *A Fireman*

The 1855 hand pump used by Penn Yan's Excelsior Company. It was the only equipment used in the earliest stages of the fire. *Courtesy of YCHC.*

Editor Stafford Cleveland of the *Chronicle* added, "Penn Yan can no longer afford to defer the purchase of a Steam Fire Engine. The case is demonstrated and we doubt whether there can be a dissenter in the village." In late June, village taxpayers voted ninety-nine to seventy-seven to purchase a Silsby Fire Steamer. It was tested by the fire department and found that it could throw water over two hundred feet.

There are two other excellent eyewitness accounts of the fire. One was written by Walter Wolcott (Penn Yan Village historian) for the fiftieth anniversary of the fire in 1922. He was twelve years old at the time of the event, had just been dismissed from the Maiden Street School for the day and was browsing the magazines at Cornwell's Bookstore on Main Street when he heard the fire alarm. His home was on Canal/Seneca Street, and he rushed home to see that his family's barn was consumed by fire and his father was working hard to save the house:

> *I remember that shortly after my father's barn burned down, I stood in the back garden of the old homestead on Canal St. and looked over towards Jacob Street. The scene that was presented to my vision could*

> *indeed be called heart-rending. Immense billows of flames were rolling up from several burning houses and over all hung a great cloud of smoke through which the sun appeared no bigger than the moon. I observed that very strenuous work was being done to save the house of Frederick Poyneer, but in spite of his efforts and his sons helped also by other men, his house caught fire and was destroyed. Soon, to my (then) unaccustomed ears came the sound of a steam fire engine in action. A stream was quickly brought to bear on the blazing ruins of Mr. Poyneer's house and the fire checked in that direction* [the Canandaigua firemen coming into the action]. *The next day Penn Yan received an influx of visitors equal to any circus day or fair time. Farmers from all parts of the county drove into town and other persons came in crowds in order to see the effects of the greatest conflagration this village had ever experienced.*[3]

The other account was written by someone in the thick of the action. Theodore Hamlin, the owner of the Metropolitan dry goods store on Main Street and a member of Keuka No. 1 fire company, wrote to his mother the day after the fire:

> *Dear Mother,*
>
> *I thought I would write a few lines this morning and tell you about the great fire we had yesterday…About 4 pm yesterday I was at work in the garden. A cart came up the street on a run with three or four men after the Head St. Engine. They cried "Fire!" and I dropped tools and everything and run* [sic] *downtown as fast as I could. I found the Furnace blazing, our engine in position and working. I at once went to the engine and worked with it until the fire was subdued. The heat became so intense that we had to withdraw our machine farther and farther from the fire, so that we could not do much execution. It was quite a long time before we got any water from the Mill to feed our machine and the Mill was our only hope as we had no place to get a drop of water except from there. Well, we worked like tigers but the wind was too much for us and everything was dry as tinder besides, so the fire spread towards Main St.…Some of these stores were entirely built of wood in the rear and only fifteen feet from a burning building. We had two streams on them then and managed to stop the fire there… As it was, the fire scorched some of the wooden ends so they were black, but our fire company saved the business part of Penn Yan. The wind blew*

very strong from the south and soon changed to southwest. Brigden's Shop was soon on fire and it spread toward the railroad with great rapidity… The firemen worked themselves almost to death and hardly anyone would relieve them. Nearly all the merchants on the east side of Main St. moved their goods and they certainly had a very narrow escape. For a while, I thought the town was doomed. Homes caught fire a long distance from the fire…There was great confusion everywhere, everyone moving and excited. The fire was all burned down at about 8 o'clock but the firemen remained on duty until well after twelve. The ruins this morning present a scene of desolation never before equaled in Penn Yan.

Hastily, your son Theodore

Their letters are in the YCHC collection.

3
THE PENN YAN MYSTERY

Leon Lewis

There are two buildings in Penn Yan today that residents would rightfully associate with St. Michael's Church, but if you go back 140 years, the people of this area would have associated both of those buildings with Leon and Harriet Lewis. What today is the rectory was the Lewis's residence, and what today houses the church offices was their horse barn. They had a print shop on the second floor of the barn, which was originally located directly behind the house. It was moved across Keuka Street in 1916 and converted into a fourteen-room home for the Sisters of St. Joseph, who taught at St. Michael's School. Walk in it today, and you would never know it was once a barn, although it was never an ordinary barn. Its construction created a bit of a stir around town. This is from the August 15, 1874 edition of the *Yates County Chronicle*:

> *If Leon Lewis Esq. does not have a nice comfortable domicile for his horses, it will be for the reason that money will not furnish it. His barn is costing more money than an ordinary church and is far more expensively furnished than a majority of such edifices. It is as elegant as a parlor and each individual horse has a large airy compartment of his own where he can range untied and free and receive the most perfect care that can be given to horseflesh. The barn is supplied with gas fixtures and the light is kept burning all night. The building will be surmounted by a handsome tower that will present a fine architectural appearance. Mr. Lewis' devotion to*

Left: The rectory of St. Michael's Church on Liberty Street, Penn Yan. *Right*: The former convent and present-day offices of St. Michael's Church on Keuka Street in Penn Yan. *Author's collection.*

his horses is only secondary to that which he gives to his library and his literary culture. His books are a marvel to behold. He has by far the most expensive and valuable collection in this quarter of the country and worth, no doubt, not less than $40,000. It embraces encyclopedias, books of travels, and works on art and literary matters in all the principle languages of Europe—French, German, Italian and Spanish as well as the choicest of English publications. A person of intelligence and literary taste would be deeply interested in the mere perusal of a catalogue of his books to say nothing of the books themselves.

Leon and Harriet Lewis didn't do anything in an ordinary way:

Their Penn Yan home on Liberty Street was lavishly furnished with costly carpeting, drapery, china, glassware, paintings and sculpture. Leon imperiled life and limb of Penn Yan residents as he dashed about the streets and roads behind blooded horses. He indulged his passion for books with an elegant

library of 25,000 volumes. Both Harriet and Leon dressed in the finest New York and imported fashions. Their entertainment was both the pleasure and the bane of Penn Yan hostesses. The ladies loved to visit or to be guests of the Lewises, but no matter how the local socialites tried, their best efforts were repeatedly outshone, not only by the magnificence of the entertaining of the pair, but by clever and unusual ways of delighting their guests.[4]

Who were Leon and Harriet Lewis and how were they able to achieve that level of comfort? Leon, whose given name was Julius Warren Lewis, was born in Connecticut in 1833. His schooling was minimal, but he loved to read and write. He published his first short story in Boston in 1852 at the age of nineteen. Around the same time, he read an article in the *Massachusetts Sabbath School Journal* written by a twelve-year old girl from Penn Yan named Harriet Newell O'Brien. He wrote to her, starting a steady exchange of correspondence between them that eventually resulted in their meeting in Penn Yan. They both loved to read and write, and they eventually fell in love and were married in 1856. Leon was twenty-three and Harriet was fifteen. It was a happy match: "Of that marriage, even the most unsympathetic observer admitted it was a union of love and that Leon and Harriet regarded each other with affection until her death."[5] It also started a prolific collaboration of writing that lasted until Harriet's death twenty-two years later.

They were prolific writers who turned out short stories, novelettes and serialized stories for major publications. It was at times difficult to know which of the two was doing the actual writing. They both used pseudonyms. Leon wrote under pen names such as "F. Clinton Barrington," "Louis Leon," "Captain Wheeler, USN" and "Illion Constellano." Harriet wrote at times under the pen names "Mrs. Grace D. Harrington," "Ernestine Hamilton" and "Mrs. Illion Constellano." Harriet on occasion wrote under Leon's name and vice versa. They wrote love stories, adventures and mysteries and sold their work to well-known publications of the time, at first the *New York Weekly* and then Robert Bonner's *New York Ledger*, by far the most widely circulated periodical in the country at the time. Leon and Harriet started writing for the *Ledger* in the 1860s, and they eventually landed lucrative contracts with the weekly periodical. In five-year contracts signed in 1868, 1873 and 1878, Leon agreed to write seventeen stories for $51,000, and Harriet agreed to write seven for $28,000. Enormous sums for the period, their earnings were what allowed them to live as well as they did in Penn Yan. Their stories were widely printed in London and translated across Europe. Harriet was touted as "the celebrated American authoress," and it was later said of Leon that he was paid more money for his stories than any writer in America.

They were at the peak of their careers and affluence in the 1870s, as evidenced by the showy barn, the Thoroughbred horses, their lavish entertainment style and a European tour they took. Leon wrote to his publisher that he was worth $150,000 in property and had $59,000 worth of insurance. Soon after they signed their third five-year contract with the *New York Ledger*, Harriet's health problems, which she had had for some time, took a turn for the worse. Leon took her to Rochester for surgery, but it did not go well. The day before she died, she wrote a letter to Robert Bonner of the *New York Ledger*: "My connection to the *Ledger* has been delightful to me. I have loved to write my stories. They have always been real to me. It costs me a pang to think that my name must die out of the familiar columns, but I can say as someone else has well said that I have never written a line which, dying, I would wish to blot." She died in May 1878 at the age of thirty-seven. For five weeks, there were tributes to her in the *Yates County Chronicle* such as this:

Leon Lewis in later years. *Northern Illinois University Libraries, Beadle and Adams Dime Novel Digitalization Project.*

Mrs. Harriet Lewis was an authoress whose name has become a household word not alone in this country but also in Europe…Although Mrs. Lewis' busy pen is now laid aside, her fertile and gifted imagination will continue to amuse and instruct the world for some time longer, as she has left behind a number of unpublished manuscripts that will be edited and put into shape for publication by her husband…The stories of this gifted lady have been republished in the English weeklies and for the last ten years the London Journal, *a weekly with a circulation of over 400,000 copies has not issued a single number without her name appearing at the head of some column. A number of her best works have been translated into various languages and met with as much success as in the original. While not possessing any absurd idea of fame, Mrs. Lewis managed in a quiet, unassuming manner not only to realize the solid comforts of life, but also to leave a name that will undoubtedly grow in renown and her stories and works will last in the minds of people long after all personal recollections of the authoress have passed away.*

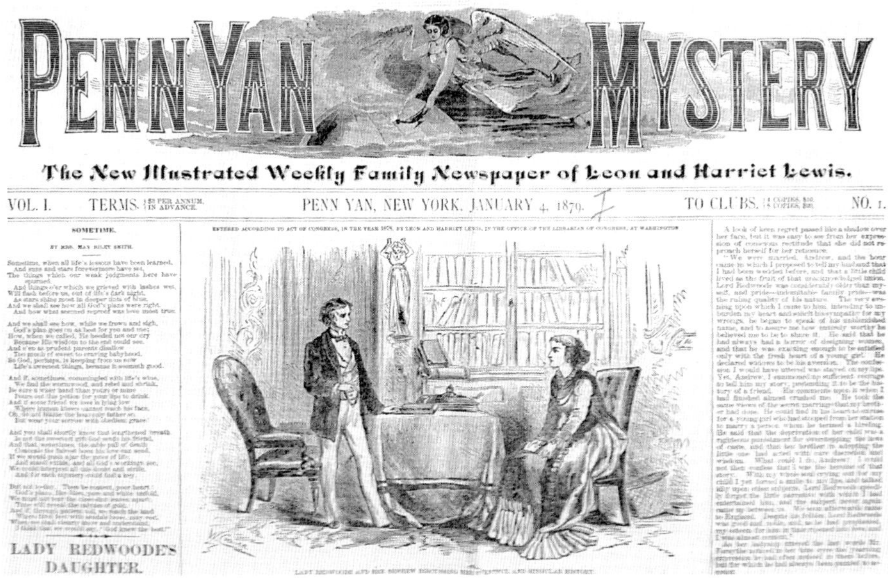

The banner of the only issue of *The Penn Yan Mystery*. *Courtesy of YCHC.*

Leon was totally devastated by Harriet's death. As he worked his way through his grief, he decided to use Harriet's unpublished manuscripts and publish a weekly periodical of his own which would compete with the *New York Ledger*. On the second floor of his horse barn, he started to assemble equipment for a sizable print shop. He threw himself into his work and, playing on his and Harriet's literary reputations, began taking subscriptions for a weekly story paper that he called the *Penn Yan Mystery*. It was advertised in newspapers across the country and promised to be an "illustrated weekly family newspaper of Leon and Harriet Lewis, 8 pages containing Stories, Voyages and Travels, Geography, Science, History and Leading Articles." Subscriptions came in from all parts of the United States.

Stafford Cleveland, editor of the *Yates County Chronicle* and a man who knew something about the pressure of putting out a weekly newspaper, issued a word of caution in his December 5, 1878 edition:

> *The first number of the* Penn Yan Mystery *shortly to be issued by Leon and Harriet Lewis is nearly ready for the press. Mr. Lewis has entered upon a gigantic enterprise and we sometimes think he has hardly counted the cost or he would not make the venture. We do not mean the money cost which*

will be very heavy, so much as the immense labor which he will impose upon himself. We know that he is a tireless and most efficient worker, but he will find in this enterprise that work will multiply on his hands beyond all previous conception. We can hardly feel doubtful however of the success of this new enterprise. Both Mr. and Mrs. Lewis have been for years making an extended reputation as writers of romance and they have many thousands of admirers and friends all over the world. Many of these friends will be eager to patronize their paper. Besides, Mr. Lewis does not need to be instructed in the art of advertising, nor to be told of the power contained in printer's ink. He is not dull in that and a right able and readable family paper may be looked for, fit in all respects for cosmopolitan circulation. And we shall not be surprised to see it rapidly attain a very large support.

The first issue went to press just before Christmas 1878 and was released on January 4, 1879. The cover story was by "Mrs. Harriet Lewis," who was also listed as coeditor, and inside was a eulogy to her written by Leon. It was widely acclaimed and promised to be a great success. The *Geneva Gazette* reported that it would be a "formidable rival" for the *New York Ledger*. The *Albany Journal* wrote, "The *Penn Yan Mystery* is the name of a new weekly illustrated paper. The mystery is how they came to start it at Penn Yan. P.S. The number before us is full of good things and argues that the enterprise is in able and experienced hands."

No other issue of the *Mystery* ever appeared. Days before the first issue was released, Leon Lewis locked the doors to his house and barn and left Penn Yan never to return. He took with him Harriet's fifteen-year-old niece and their adopted daughter, Julia Wheelock, whose parents had gone west to Wisconsin. Leon told friends that they were going Christmas shopping in Rochester when they boarded the train in Penn Yan. It was the middle of January before it became known that Leon and his "daughter" were gone. On January 16, 1879, the *Chronicle* reported:

Leon Lewis—That this noted gentleman is no longer a citizen of Penn Yan seems now to be a settled fact. On New Years Day, it is said, he was seen by a citizen of this village to go on board the ocean steamer Scythia *bound for Liverpool. The passenger list embraced the names of L. Lewis and Miss Lewis. The latter was the adopted daughter of himself and wife, about fourteen years old* [sic], *a niece of Mrs. Leon Lewis. Previous to his departure nine heavy trunks were sent to New York containing such articles as he had chosen to pack and carry with him. The motive for his flight is*

> *still somewhat of a mystery...But he was a restless spirit and ill content with the ordinary conditions of life. He longed for greater notoriety and was not content to labor and to wait. Patience was not his highest virtue.*

Many explanations were offered for this inexplicable action but the one most commonly agreed on was that Leon had accrued massive debts and was in serious financial difficulty. It was said that he had debts exceeding $50,000. One could also assume that a love affair (he and Julia were soon married in England) between a forty-six-year-old man and his fifteen-year-old niece/adopted daughter so soon after Harriet's death would be difficult for Penn Yan society to accept.

Two months after he left town, Leon wrote a letter from England to editor Cleveland of the *Chronicle*. He asked to be sent a bill for printing jobs and explained that he had taken care of portions of his indebtedness by deeding over houses that he owned on Maiden Lane and elsewhere in the village, left his furniture for auction and the same with his library, which he valued between $20,000 and $30,000. He explained that he had a contract in his hands with the *New York Ledger* worth $56,000. At the end he asked, "Who[m], therefore, have I plundered? Who is injured by my departure? Whose business is it that I have abandoned the *Mystery*, as long as I pay all obligations contracted therein?" His home and barn on Liberty Street and other real estate were taken over by those who held the mortgages. His furniture and the contents of his barn were sold at public auction. His library of twenty-five thousand books was sold at a public book sale held over three days and netting $1,500.

There was general bewilderment over why Leon Lewis left town. The *Chronicle* on April 4, 1879 reported, "The residue and remnants of the personal property of Leon Lewis were sold at auction last week...Mr. Lewis had expended large sums of money in furnishing his place with every facility and convenience for comfort...How a man could provide so much to make a perfect home and deliberately flee away from it is something of a Mystery truly. Perhaps some day he will be good enough to give a solution to this strange mystery." Then there was this story in the *Chronicle* a little earlier: "From the *Lyons Republican*—'We could almost be reconciled to the departure of Leon Lewis and the blotting out of his *Mystery* if he would write home and tell us how he got that girl out of the scrape he got her into in the opening chapter of his last story.'" The *Chronicle* asked, "Would it not be quite as interesting to learn how he proposed to retrieve himself from the very bad scrape in which he has involved himself? To let the girl in the story out would be a mighty deal easier task for him."

Leon and Julia lived in London, England, for five years, where they had two children. Leon continued to make a living with his pen, writing stories for boy's magazines. He and his family returned to the United States in 1884, living on Long Island for a while, then Dubuque, Iowa, and Chicago. In Chicago, Leon wrote for the city's newspapers and continued to write fiction for periodicals. He also wrote several dime novels for the House of Beadle & Adams. He moved back to New York City in 1897 to write for the *New York World*. He and Julia were divorced in 1913. She remarried, but Leon went to live with his sister in Bakersville, Connecticut, where he died by his own hand in 1920 at the age of eighty-seven.

4

LEON LEWIS REVISITED

Another Penn Yan Mystery

The years following the end of the Civil War saw a major expansion of railroad construction around the country. The war had proven the advantages of being able to move goods and people rapidly by rail. The war had also produced a class of wealthy businessmen in the North with political clout, money to invest and a desire to grow their businesses. Every city and small town in America saw a railroad connection as the key to its future growth. America's first transcontinental railroad, the Union Pacific, was completed in 1869. Construction on Canada's first transcontinental railroad was begun in 1871 and continued throughout that decade. In the 1870s, every town in Yates County was trying to figure out how to connect onto one railroad line or another. This environment produced many schemes for railroad construction throughout the country.

Years before Leon Lewis left Penn Yan forever, he enhanced his reputation as a visionary by developing a plan to build a railroad across Mexico, from the Yucatán Peninsula on the Caribbean to Acapulco on the Pacific, which he called the Mexican Pacific Railroad. He planned a second railroad starting from Yucatán and going southeast through Central America to the Pacific Coast in Costa Rica.

This article originally appeared in the *Tonawanda Herald* in March of 1877 and was reprinted in the *Yates County Chronicle*:

> *Mr. Leon Lewis, the distinguished author, bids fair to acquire greater distinction as a "railroad king" than he has in the field of literature. He*

> *appears as the projector and builder of two great international railways which are to traverse the southern states of Mexico and the Republics of Central America. The first of these roads is the Mexican Pacific and the other the Central American. Both roads start from Ciudad Yucatan, a new seaport with an excellent harbor founded by Mr. Lewis in the northeast corner of Yucatan. The Mexican Pacific skirts along the southern shore of the Gulf of Mexico, unites with a branch from the Cordilleras, to Acapulco on the Pacific coast. This is said to be just a thousand miles from one terminus to the other. The new roads will open up a hitherto undeveloped country of fabulous wealth and vast natural resources and Mr. Lewis offers great inducements to emigrants from all parts of the world to settle along these lines. Those who are interested in the matter will do well to address Mr. Lewis at Penn Yan N.Y.*

In March 1877, Leon Lewis sat down with Stafford Cleveland, the editor of the *Yates County Chronicle*, for an in-depth interview about his railroad scheme. He explained that he had connections with General Santa Anna of Mexico going back to 1866. Santa Anna was living in exile in Staten Island and (according to Lewis) wrote to him asking him to concoct a plan to oust Emperor Maximilian from Mexico so he could once again assume power. Lewis told Santa Anna that he could never accomplish anything with the military leaders that surrounded him. He said that the Mexican generals "were not fit to be corporals." In the 1870s, the Mexican government was again in turmoil, and Lewis said that it didn't matter who ran Mexico—his scheme was too valuable not to be backed by the government.

He explained to the editor that the Suez Canal, because of its location, would soon be filled in with shifting desert sands and Europeans would be looking for another route to Asia. He believed that his railroad route would be more valuable than around the Cape of Good Hope (Africa) or across Panama because of the vast financial potential of Mexican resources. He said that the route he had planned across Mexico traversed rich cotton land and mountains with huge deposits of gold, silver, copper, coal and quicksilver. He spelled out a few additional benefits of his railroad, including encouraging immigration to Mexico from Europe and elsewhere. Another result of his railroad would be the restoration of Mexico's native tribes (in particular, the Mayans and Aztecs) to the glory and preeminence of the past.

When he was asked how he intended to finance construction, Lewis said that he had enough of his own finances to build the first hundred miles. The bulk of the project would be financed by fifty-seven-mile-wide land grants from the

MEXICAN PACIFIC
and
Central American Railways

LEON LEWIS
Projector, Builder and Proprietor

Another Great March of Civilization

Mexico and Central America Furnishing the one Supreme Route of Travel and Commerce Between North and South America

Europe and Asia Clasping Hands Across Mexico

The Twin Highways of the Nations North and South and East and West

The Grandest Project of our Day or Generation

A New Epoch Dawning Upon Mexico and Central America

(Headlines in the ***Yates County Chronicle*** *March 29, 1877)*

Left: Headlines in the March 29, 1877 issue of the *Yates County Chronicle. Author's collection.*

Opposite: Map from the March 29, 1877 issue of the *Yates County Chronicle. Author's collection.*

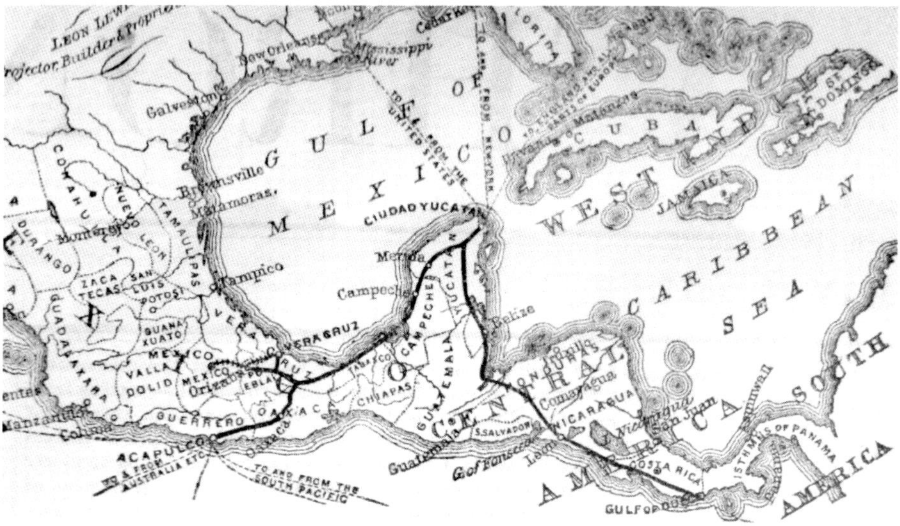

Mexican government for a right of way. He believed that the Mexican railroad would be built within five years, and then, 90 percent of all business between Europe and Asia would pay a toll to Mexico by using his railway. Sales of the granted land, with its rich financial potential, would provide more than enough money for construction. Land then worth three cents an acre would jump to one hundred dollars an acre. Lewis told the editor:

> *I will say nothing of these things. If I did, I would have the whole human race around me, revolvers in hand, demanding to be taken in as partners, and I couldn't do it! The fact is I don't want a dollar of anybody. If you say anything about my projects in the* Chronicle, *make the fact plain to everybody: I don't want a dollar. The work upon which I have entered will produce the cash as fast as I want it. The thing I do want is a million good families from Europe and America to go down there and become rich and happy—and this is a matter to which I am giving my attention.*

When asked by editor Cleveland why he was not afraid that someone like railroad magnate Jay Gould would take the project away from him, he responded:

> *I am the only man living who can build the roads in question in our generation. There has got to be a MAN at the head of this enterprise who can be found at all hours of the day or night by anyone having financial*

> *claims—a man who has the brains to conceive his roads in accordance with the predestinations of the Almighty; the heart to carry his plans out in love to the nation of today and to posterity; and a sound business capacity by which he can make himself respected by the great money kings of Europe. I am not going to blow my own trumpet, but I freely tell you I am the man for this business. Besides, I say of it what Napoleon said when he assumed the iron crown of Charlemagne: "God has given it to me; let him beware who would touch it."...The prospectus—which will now soon be ready for distribution—will contain hundreds of official letters from the great men of the world including emperors, kings, presidents, cardinals—Such a host as few men ever have for correspondents. All these letters convey to me the heartiest approbation and faith of their writers and why shouldn't they? A man must be weak-minded not to see at a glance that I am a man of destiny and that in building the Mexican Pacific, I am simply carrying out a decree of the Almighty.*

Lewis did indeed send out an eight-page prospectus, printed in both English and Spanish and including the map used in this chapter. He sent it mainly to newspapers around the country as far away as California and Hawaii. The reactions, which were reprinted in subsequent issues of the *Chronicle*, were glowing:

> *Mr. Lewis asserts that this route is superior to any other between the eastern and western hemispheres. That is to say it will by its advantages take precedence over the Suez route, the Union Pacific Railroad, the Cape of Good Hope, or the Panama railroad or canal. The ports at either terminus are the finest in the world, where the largest ships can ride safely at anchor amidst the wildest storms.*
>
> Elmira Daily Advertiser, *April 19, 1877*

> *The fame of Leon Lewis of Penn Yan as an author is worldwide, but he is now engaged in a gigantic railway enterprise which if successful—and success appears not only possible, but very probable—will place him at the head of the practical thinkers and doers of the age.*
>
> Progressive Batavian, *Batavia, New York*

> *The attention of the readers of the* Journal *is specially directed to an article elsewhere in reference to the Mexican Pacific Railroad. Mr. Leon Lewis, the distinguished author and literateur is commending himself to the*

> *people of the South by his earnestness in behalf of this grand highway. We can conceive of no enterprise of more abiding interest to Southern men than the Mexican Pacific Railroad. Much of the future of our section depends upon this road and the sooner we grasp the situation and master it, the sooner will our prosperity be assured.*
>
> Montgomery (Alabama) State Journal

> *We give some extracts from the press in regard to the great project originating in the great mind of Leon Lewis of Penn Yan. That village may well be proud that it is the home of the originator of so grand a scheme.*
>
> Hammondsport Herald

There was also some skepticism:

> *The* Penn Yan Chronicle *comes to us this week with a three-column account of Leon Lewis's scheme for a great "Mexican Pacific Railway." We have heard of Mr. and Mrs. Lewis as great travelers and renowned novelists whose stories have been published in an excellent weekly paper for ten years past and found admirers in thousands of homes. The railway "project" is evidently another flight of his brilliant imagination which, instead of increasing his renown and well-earned fame, is likely to land him at Willard on Seneca Lake rather than his pictured home near the Gulf of Mexico. If Yates were not an anti-license* [no legal sale of alcohol] *county, we would assume that the party to this magnificent scheme was quite drunk, and that our estimable friend, Bro. Cleveland of the* Chronicle *had been imbibing from the same vial or smelling his breath.*
>
> Geneva Gazette, *May 11, 1877*

What happened to the scheme? The simple answer is nothing. Was Leon Lewis playing a joke on the *Chronicle* and everyone else? Was it a pipe dream that he never carried out? Was he distracted by his wife's serious illness and death? Did the turmoil in Mexico scuttle the plan? The fact is that there is no further mention of it in the *Yates County Chronicle* after May 1, 1877. I read through each issue until the summer of 1879, months after Leon Lewis left Penn Yan and the country. There was not a single mention of the railroad plan in the *New York Times*. Thanks to Google books, I looked through four different books on the history of railroads in Mexico and did not find a single reference to Leon Lewis. The Mexican Pacific Railway was eventually built, but at a different time, along a different route and by different people.

Leon Lewis's "railroad scheme" is indeed a mystery. The *Auburn Morning News* of January 14, 1879, reported:

> *Leon Lewis, the great novelist, the distinguished writer, the millionaire, the "projector, builder and proprietor" of the Mexican Pacific Railway, the editor, proprietor and publisher of the* Penn Yan Mystery, *and the great modern humbug, has collapsed. On the first of January, Lewis sailed from New York on the* Scythia *for Europe, leaving behind a goodly number of creditors.*
>
> *He was a man of great pretensions and unlimited cheek, indulging in eccentricities that reflected seriously upon his sanity. He lived in great extravagance, being the leader in fashion and the admiration of those who bow at the shrine of pretentious arrogance. But all is changed now. Everyone knew him to be a pretentious snob, although a good story writer. His fine horses, rich carriages and elaborate accompaniments, his diamonds, jewels, valuable statuary, velvet carpets, his $20,000 library, the* Penn Yan Mystery *and the great Mexican Railway scheme have all vanished.*

5

PENN YAN'S WHALE TALE

In May 2000, noted author Nathaniel Philbrick, who lives on Nantucket Island, published a book titled *In the Heart of the Sea*. The book spent forty weeks on the *New York Times* bestseller list and won the 2000 National Book Award for Nonfiction. It told the story of the Nantucket whaling ship *Essex* that was on an expedition in the South Pacific in November 1820 when it was rammed by an eighty-five-foot-long sperm whale and sunk. The crew of twenty got into three whaling boats and planned to row to the coast of South America, a voyage they estimated would take fifty-six days. It became a desperate struggle for survival for the crew members. One by one, men succumbed to starvation and exposure and the survivors eventually resorted to cannibalism of those who perished. Only eight members of the crew lived to be picked up three months later by another whaling ship. They never made it to the shores of South America. Shortly after his rescue and return to Nantucket, First Mate Owen Chase wrote an account of his experiences onboard the *Essex*. It was a copy of that account that later inspired a young Massachusetts author, Herman Melville, in the writing of his most famous novel, *Moby-Dick*, which was published in 1851.

So what does all that have to do with Penn Yan? In the preface of *In the Heart of the Sea*, Nathaniel Philbrick wrote:

> *For nearly 180 years, most of what was known about the calamity came from the 128-page* Narrative of the Wreck of the Whaleship *Essex, written by Owen Chase, the ship's first mate. Fragmentary accounts from*

Illustration from Raul Literature Weblog.

Opposite: The residence in Penn Yan where the manuscript was kept in the attic for eighty-two years. *Author's collection.*

other survivors existed, but these lacked the authority and scope of Chase's narrative, which was published with the help of a ghostwriter only nine months after the first mate's rescue. Then, around 1960, an old notebook was found in the attic of a home in Penn Yan, New York. Not until twenty years later, in 1980, when the notebook reached the hands of the Nantucket whaling expert Edouard Stackpole, was it realized that its original owner, Thomas Nickerson, had been the Essex*'s cabin boy.*

That touched off a few phone calls to the Penn Yan Public Library, which were fielded by reference librarian John Creamer and local history specialist Joanie Hand. People wanted to know the details: Where in Penn Yan was the manuscript found? Who had it? How did they get it? John Creamer contacted the Nantucket Historical Association and found out that the story of the manuscript was a bit more complex than originally thought.

The 105-page manuscript was written in 1876, fifty-six years after the Essex was sunk. At the time Nickerson wrote his account, he was running a boardinghouse on Nantucket. One of his summertime boarders was the same Leon Lewis of Penn Yan mentioned in the two previous chapters. Upon hearing of Nickerson's account of the incident onboard the *Essex*, Leon Lewis talked him into letting him take the manuscript back to Penn Yan so he could edit it and get it ready for publication. Upon returning to Penn Yan, Lewis's life became somewhat chaotic. His wife Harriet became desperately ill and eventually died in 1878 and Lewis channeled all his energies into his publication, *The Penn Yan Mystery*. Then came his abrupt disappearance from Penn Yan with his niece. With the death of Thomas Nickerson on Nantucket in 1883, the manuscript was totally forgotten.

A sheriff's sale of Leon Lewis's property in Penn Yan was held to pay off some of his creditors. Before the sale, a good friend of Lewis, Darius A. Ogden, was able to get possession of several items of value, including Nickerson's manuscript. Ogden, a prominent local politician and orator, lived on the corner of Clinton and Hamilton Streets in Penn Yan, which is where the manuscript stayed until 1960. It was passed down through the Ogden family along with the house. It was there that it was discovered in the attic by Ann W. Finch, who took it home with her to Hamden, Connecticut. She kept it in a box in her study for another twenty years. She thought the story was fantasy: "The story seemed a little far-fetched to me. I thought it was copied by some sea-struck young man who read it someplace and wanted a copy of it for himself." After a summer vacation to Nantucket in 1980, she decided to send it to the Nantucket Historical Society to see if it was authentic. After analysis, the society members who analyzed the manuscript realized its historical significance. It was published by the Nantucket Historical Association using Nickerson's original title, *The Loss of the Ship "Essex" Sunk by a Whale and the Ordeal of the Crew in Open Boats*. That was in 1984, 108 years after Thomas Nickerson handed it over to Leon Lewis for that purpose. In 1986, Nathaniel Philbrick moved to Nantucket and became interested in the history of the island and the whaling industry in particular. Since the publication of *In the Heart of the Sea*, Philbrick has become a very prolific writer. But for this one book, at any rate, there was a definite Penn Yan connection.

6

THE STRANGE CASE OF COUNTY TREASURER JAMES BURNS

Defaulting bank cashiers and faithless public servants of all kinds are so common nowadays that it would seem that honest officials are the exception rather than the rule. Probably an instance of betrayed trust, presenting sad results almost unparalleled, is that of the defaulting Treasurer of Yates County.
New York Herald, *March 7, 1873*

The decade following the end of the Civil War is often seen as the beginning of a golden age of government corruption. Reconstruction in the South, the boom in railroad construction, accelerated industrial growth, rapid urbanization and a severe drought of quality political leadership at all levels of government provided easy opportunities for unscrupulous men to enrich themselves at public expense. From the scandals of the Grant administration, railroad scandals in Congress (Credit Mobilier), statewide political machines in industrialized states and city bosses like Boss Tweed in New York, corruption was rampant. Yates County was not immune.

Take the strange case of James Burns of Penn Yan. Burns was born in Massachusetts in 1827. Around the age of twenty, he married Cornelia Cummings of New Jersey and, shortly after that, left for California in search of gold, one of the "Forty-Niners." He experienced some success out there and came east to Penn Yan around 1850. Once here, he bought in as a partner in a bookstore, entered the book trade and became quite prosperous. He and Cornelia had four sons, all born in Penn Yan. He built a stately home on a large lot at the corner of Benham and Jacob Streets that just barely escaped the disastrous fire of 1872. (Part of that building now houses the VFW.) He became a member of the Masons and the Odd Fellows. During the Civil War, he was elected captain of Yates County's home guard unit, the Excelsior Guards. He was described as tall, extremely personable and alarmingly handsome, so it was natural that he should gravitate toward local politics. He was elected county treasurer in 1860 and again every three years through 1869. He was, in short, a model citizen and businessman, a pillar of the community. Then, when his last term expired in 1872, he inexplicably abandoned his wife and children, absconded with $42,000 of taxpayers' money and left town with a younger woman with whom he had been carrying on an affair. It then appeared that he had disappeared off the face of the earth.

I had intended to write this entire article myself, but in doing the research for it, I ran across an article written by an unnamed local correspondent and published in the *New York Times* on March 8, 1873. It is better than anything I could have done.

> *A Sad Case: The Story of the Defaulting Treasurer of Yates County*
> *The* New York Times*—March 8, 1873*
> *Penn Yan NY—Crime in high life affords a more interesting chapter in the narration than that committed in circles where it is the more natural to expect moral delinquencies and disrespect of law, both human and divine. Hence transgressions, the recital of which but a passing remark in the one case, are devoured in minutest detail and become food for extended and bitter comment in the other.*
>
> *This village and county are now in the midst of intense excitement over the return to Penn Yan, in the custody of the sheriff, of a man who a short time since was a member of the best society of the place and whose family was a model of respectability and culture. He was the Treasurer of the county and had been for twelve years in succession and possessed the unbounded confidence of the entire community. He became a defaulter, however, in a large amount to the county and the State, and absconded nearly a year ago in company with a young woman who had also been recognized as a member of the best society, leaving behind him, disgraced and ruined, a wife and three children. The case is one of unusual interest, owing to the standing of the parties concerned, and to its singular denouement.*
>
> *The man referred to is James N. Burns. The lady is Miss Cynthia Cooley, who was left an orphan a few years since, which, and the subsequent decease of an uncle who willed her his property, left her very comfortably*

provided for. She was also the possessor of beauty and accomplishments. Her parents dying, and there being minor children, Mr. Burns was selected as the most proper person to be made the guardian of the children and the executor of the estate. This was five years ago. In performing the duties incumbent upon him in the relations he held toward the Cooleys, Burns became a slave to the charms of Miss Cooley and an attachment that culminated in the ruin of both was the result. Burns sacrificed the happiness of his family and respect and confidence of his friends upon the altar of his unholy passion; and for Burns, Miss Cooley delivered up her honor as a woman, her standing in society, and became an outcast and a fugitive from justice.

In May last, the intimacy between Burns and Miss Cooley still existing, and they being absent together for weeks at a time, the sureties on Burns' bond seeing that his fall was complete, urged the Board of Supervisors to make an examination into his accounts. The matter was delayed for the time, but Burns took the alarm and in the early part of the above month he went away, saying that he was going to Rhode Island on a visit to some friends. He left a letter with his clerk with instructions to deliver it to Judge Briggs, one of his bondsmen, if he should not return before the last of June. A few days after Burns went away, Miss Cooley also disappeared. This gave rise to considerable remarks and looked very suspicious. The last of June having arrived, and no tidings of Burns, the letter in the charge of the clerk at the treasurer's office was delivered to Judge Briggs. Its contents revealed the fact that the worse fears of Burns' friends were more than realized. He confessed to being a defaulter in the amount of $38,090 and that he had left Penn Yan never to return. He said that he took all the blame of his action upon himself, but plead his unhappy family affairs as influencing him in a great degree. He granted to Judge Briggs a power of attorney to settle up his affairs and to apply the proceeds of his effects toward the liquidation of his indebtedness, thus virtually leaving his family destitute. Those who had known the noble-minded, honorable James Burns of five years ago were loth [sic] *to believe that he had sunk to such depths of degradation, but his letter could not be denied, and an examination of his books revealed even a larger defalcation than confessed—about $42,000.*

Nothing could be found giving any clue to the whereabouts of the fugitives and all efforts to apprehend them were abandoned after a short time. On the 3rd of February last, Sheriff John D. Dinturff of this county was surprised to receive a dispatch from the Police Superintendent of San

Francisco, California stating that James Burns, the defaulting Treasurer of Yates County, was in San Francisco. How any information as to Burns had come to the knowledge of those authorities was more than the Sheriff could understand, but he made arrangements to proceed at once to California and so informed the Chief of Police.

It seems that a few years since a gentleman named Lawrence removed from Penn Yan to San Francisco. In the latter part of January last this gentleman met Burns on the street in that city. He had not seen Burns since he left Penn Yan and although the fugitive was in a measure disguised by a change in the style of his beard and presented an old, haggard, and care-worn appearance, Lawrence recognized him, and being acquainted with the facts of his defalcation, determined to find out where he was stopping. He followed Burns to the Brooklyn House. Thinking that there might possibly be a doubt as to the identity of Burns, and feeling certain if it was him, Cynthia Cooley would be in his company, Lawrence informed a man named Lee of the discovery he had probably made. Lee was also a resident of Yates County and well acquainted with Miss Cooley. He therefore accompanied Mr. Lawrence to the hotel. They met Burns and with him a female whom Lee recognized at once as the paramour of the defaulting Treasurer. He called Miss Cooley by name but she, with remarkable presence of mind, paid no attention to him. He then forced himself upon her notice. When she became indignant and assured him that he was entirely mistaken in the person. Such unblushing coolness rather staggered Mr. Lee and he began to think he might be mistaken, when Burns commenced weeping compulsively and exclaimed "I told you so, Cynthia! I knew they would find us at last!" Miss Cooley manifested apparently no emotion and retired to her apartments. Lee and Lawrence informed the police authorities, with the result stated. [Lee and Lawrence were tipped off by Darius Ogden of Penn Yan, one of Burns's bondsmen, who also supplied them with photos of the two fugitives.]

Sheriff Dinturff started for San Francisco on the 12th of February, arrived there on the 20th, obtained a requisition from Gov. Booth, although Burns said he would accompany the Sheriff without a requisition, and arrived here with his prisoner on Saturday last. Miss Cooley left for the East before the Sheriff reached San Francisco. She was arrested at Elmira on her arrival there but subsequently released and is now in that city. Burns was admitted to bail in the sum of $2000.

Expecting great excitement in Penn Yan when he should arrive here with Burns, the time of his arrival was kept secret and Burns was conveyed to the hotel before word spread. In less than five minutes thereafter, the Benham House was surrounded by hundreds of curious citizens, anxious to get a sight of the defaulter. On reaching the hotel, one of Burns' sons was waiting to greet him. As soon as Burns saw his boy, he uttered a cry of joy, as he had not anticipated meeting any of those he had so shamefully abandoned, and breaking from the Sheriff, he caught his son to his bosom and pressed kisses fast and thick upon his face, while his frame shook with the most convulsive sobs. The kind-hearted Sheriff, bathed in tears, was forced to tear the father and son apart and locked Burns up in a room by himself.

When the Sheriff entered Burns' cell in San Francisco, the unhappy man, choking with emotion, exclaimed, "Thank God, Sheriff! You've come! I'm so glad! I'm so glad!" He then fell into violent convulsions from which he was relieved with great difficulty. At Chicago another affecting scene in this sad drama was enacted. The oldest son of Burns is a telegraph operator in that city and had read every message that passed over the wires concerning his father and knew the exact condition of affairs. He met the party at the depot and was allowed to see and converse with his father for several hours.

Burns, upon leaving Penn Yan, went to New York. Here he was joined by Miss Cooley. They first went to Central America and from there to Europe, visiting England, Ireland, Wales, and other countries. Leaving Europe, they went to Barbados and the Sandwich Islands and on the 10th of January landed in California. Burns told Sheriff Dinturff that, so overwhelmed was he with remorse, that he had not passed a peaceful or happy moment since he absconded, until he knew he was in custody. He could not rid himself of the idea in all his wanderings that he was destined to be captured and brought to punishment. He felt unspeakable relief when he was arrested.

After the scene between Burns and his son at the Benham House here, the former became delirious and is now in critical condition. He has been taken to the residence of his brother-in-law, where he is being attended by his wife, whose just resentment and bitterness toward her faithless husband has all been dispelled by the sight of his wretched state. As soon as he is able, Burns will answer proceedings in bankruptcy. After all his estate is turned in against the claims against him, his sureties (bondsmen) will be compelled to make good about $24,000.

DENOUEMENT

Jim Burns was well connected in county politics and had powerful friends in Penn Yan. In April 1873, he was indicted by a grand jury on two counts. The first was "for neglect to perform duties assigned by act of the legislature" and the other "for neglect to perform his official duties" to which pleas of not guilty were entered. His bail was fixed by the court at $10,000. However, he never stood trial, was never convicted and never did prison time. Instead, his debt was settled by a variety of means. A bill was introduced in Albany to forgive the part of the $42,000 that belonged to the state. The county legislature lowered the amount of their claim against him by $1,000. He filed for bankruptcy, and the sale of his property in Penn Yan and investments he held were used as a part of the settlement. In the end, his bondsmen from his days as treasurer (all powerful, wealthy businessmen in the community) put up the difference. In January 1874, the county legislature met and agreed that the debt incurred by Burns's theft had been settled. The *Yates County Chronicle* at the time reported:

> *We are heartily glad the settlement has been effected. It is due very much to the exertions of Mr. Burns himself that it has been accomplished. And he is entitled to credit for his good management in bringing it to completion. A fair survey of all the facts ought to soften in a very considerable degree the harsh judgment the public was inclined for some time to pronounce in this case... We have always been thankful that with the power to take so much, he took so little.*

Shortly after that, Jim Burns, to the complete surprise of everyone, again left town. He picked up Cynthia Cooley in Elmira, and they traveled together to Salt Lake City, Utah, where they were married in February 1875. In the spring of 1879, he and Cynthia left Salt Lake City and, after a trip on horseback of four hundred miles that lasted nineteen days, ended up in a newly developed mining community (Challis) along the Lost River in Idaho. He wrote back to Editor Stafford Cleveland of the *Yates County Chronicle* (who was one of his bondsmen.): "This Idaho is a wonderful country and its prospects for being a great silver and gold producing country are not equaled [*sic*] on this side of the Rocky Mountains. I hope to make a strike here this summer and will put you in a mine; that is if I strike a good one. I shall remember Yates County if I ever strike a good thing here." He made enough money from mining to start up a hotel in Challis, the Burns House. Toward the end of 1883, Cynthia Cooley Burns died of pneumonia and

The Yates County Courthouse Park as it was in the 1870s. The courthouse is to the left and the clerk's office building to the right. *Courtesy of YCHC.*

Burns married for a third time. He became, once again, a pillar of the community and was elected probate judge in 1887. He held that post until his death.

Reading through the newspaper accounts of the time, there is a tendency to be somewhat sympathetic toward Jim Burns. Sheriff Dinturff mentioned that Burns fell off a scaffold while prospecting during the gold rush in California: "This caused an injury to his head which made him at times to be subject to crazy spells, the symptoms of which were violent and often ridiculous actions." This apparently manifested itself during times of stress. The chief of police in San Francisco noted Burns's behavior in a telegram to Sheriff Dinturff at the time he arrested Burns: "Arrested Burns. He wants to go at once, without requisition. He has fits, acts crazy. Will require two men to take charge of him. I can send men if arrangements can be made by you for passage and necessary expenses on road. Woman will go with him. Answer quick." On another occasion, Dinturff himself observed the condition. When the great fire broke out in Penn Yan in 1872, the sheriff rushed to the Northern Central Railroad station to send out a telegram for assistance: "As I passed by Mr. Burns' residence, I observed the county treasurer on the front lawn and he was having a crazy spell of the most outrageously violent nature."

The fire of 1872 may have been the catalyst for Burn's actions. His house on Jacob Street was slightly damaged by the fire, and Cynthia's house, which was directly across the street, was totally destroyed. The fire occurred on April 30, and he left town with Cynthia and the county funds exactly two weeks later.

It is somewhat difficult to feel sympathy toward Cynthia Cooley. The story in the *New York Herald* quoted at the top of this article described her: "She was a remarkably beautiful young lady, a blond, and highly accomplished withal." The article emphasized that Burns was overwhelmed by guilt the whole time they were traveling together:

> *He landed in San Francisco a heart-broken cheerless man. In all his wanderings…he was haunted by the thought that he was pursued. He had a perpetual longing to return to Penn Yan and give himself up, but was restrained by his paramour. He said that he never ceased to believe that he would, sooner or later, be apprehended and arrived at that stage that he was impatient of the delay in justice overtaking him. The happiest moment he experienced since he left Penn Yan was that when he saw Sheriff Dinturff enter his cell and knew that at last the dreadful suspense was over.*

The article in the *Herald* ended by mentioning that Cynthia's younger sister, Lucy Cooley of Elmira, did the same thing in that city. She went west with a man who abandoned his wife and three children.

The most sympathetic person in this episode would have to be the abandoned wife of Jim Burns, Cornelia. When Burns was brought back from San Francisco, she said that she would be willing to forgive her wayward husband and Cynthia if he would come back to her. When he and Cynthia left for good in 1874, Cornelia sold their house on Jacob Street in Penn Yan and bought a farm in Maryland with her brother. She died in 1911, and her obituary referred to her as "the widow of James Burns," which would indicate that there was never a divorce and explains why Burns married Cynthia in Utah. She is buried in Lakeview Cemetery in Penn Yan alongside two of their sons who had died young. In 1888, a third son died in Chicago, and Jim Burns brought his remains to Penn Yan to be buried with his brothers and mother. When he returned to Idaho, he sent an open letter to be printed in the *Chronicle*. In it, he wrote:

> *Thirty-eight years ago, I came to Penn Yan a stranger to make this town my home. With kind and loving words I was then received. Fourteen years ago I left for the West to make a new home for myself and now on my return to visit you, I find your hearts warm toward me, your kind words of welcome are dearer to me than language can express. I return to my home in Idaho feeling that in Yates County, I have a host of true and earnest friends, and that I may be worthy of your friendship is my earnest desire.*

He died in Idaho two years later at the age of sixty-three. His obituary, printed in the *Yates County Chronicle*, ended: "It cannot be denied that he had weaknesses incident to human life, but let him who is without fault cast the first stone. Peace to his ashes."

7

KEUKA LAKE'S STEAMBOAT WARS

One doesn't normally associate the peaceful waters of Keuka Lake with any kind of war, but as the era of the steamboat entered its golden age in the decades following the Civil War, there were three of them. Each "war" was actually a struggle for dominance between competing companies on the lake. This was a time when men in business and finance amassed large fortunes throughout the economy by using cutthroat competition to create monopolies. Steamboat companies on Keuka Lake did not escape that type of competition.

The first steamboat war was in 1873 and resulted in the domination of commerce on the lake by the Lake Keuka Steam Navigation Co., jointly owned by Joseph Crosby, Farley Holmes and Morris F. Sheppard. As agricultural production around the lake increased and as the Northern Central Railroad and the Bath & Hammondsport Railroad brought increased numbers of "excursionists" to its shores for recreation, competition between the steamboat companies returned in the late 1870s. The Lake Keuka Steam Navigation Co. was basically Penn Yan oriented and based its schedule around the Northern Central Railroad. The new company formed in 1877 was Hammondsport oriented and based its schedule around the Bath & Hammondsport Railroad. This touched off the second steamboat war. With newer and more preferred steamboats (the *Lulu* and the *Urbana*), the new company took business away from the older one. The death of Farley Holmes in 1879, consecutive seasons of financial loss and storm damage to their aging flagship (the *Steuben*) resulted in the dissolution of the Lake Keuka

Steam Navigation Co. in 1881. The victorious company reorganized and looked forward to enjoying their monopoly of commerce on the lake. That included raising freight rates and ticket prices to make up for the low rates they had been forced to charge because of earlier competition.

Into this scene came William L. Halsey. Halsey was born and raised in Steuben County but went west as a young man and made his fortune in railroads and steamboats in the Pacific Northwest. (There is a town in Oregon named after him.) He returned to New York in the 1870s and lived in Rochester. There he got involved in various business enterprises and a law practice, all of which added to his wealth. He bought land on Keuka Lake and built a large cottage near the Grove Spring Hotel named Care Naught. There he developed a friendship with Farley Holmes and, because of that, closely followed the second "boat war" of the late 1870s. Troubled by the shabby treatment of Holmes's widow by the new company, Halsey started buying stock in the Lake Keuka Navigation Co. and won a seat on its board of directors. As the story goes, he was incensed one stormy night in 1882 when the *Urbana* refused to stop at his dock at Care Naught. He confronted Morris Sheppard (who by then was an officer in the company) on the street in Penn Yan and said to him, "If you can't operate this boat to accommodate the public, I'll build one of my own!" Sheppard's response was: "You couldn't build a rowboat!" And that started the third and final steamboat war.

Halsey allied himself with some powerful Penn Yan businessmen: Theodore O. Hamlin, who ran the Metropolitan, a dry goods store on Main Street; Oliver C. Knapp, who ran a downtown hotel; and William Wise of Hollowell & Wise Hardware. They formed the Crooked Lake Navigation Company and hired Alonzo Springstead to build an elegant state-of-the-art steamboat, which Halsey named the *Farley Holmes* after his friend. The competition started in earnest when the *Holmes* was launched at Hammondsport in July 1883. The maiden voyage included guests personally invited by Halsey. A special dinner was held at the Grove Springs Hotel and then the *Holmes* proceeded north to enter the outlet and dock at Penn Yan. The "new line" (Halsey's company) had leased a dock near the steamboat landings, but there were rumors that there might be a confrontation with workers from the "old line." The county sheriff was on hand with twenty-five deputies in case they were needed. A large crowd gathered on both sides of the outlet to see the new boat and watch what happened as it tried to dock. The *Holmes*'s dock had one of the "old line" boats tied up to it, but once it was removed, the *Holmes* was allowed to dock without incident.

Left: Penn Yan banker Morris F. Sheppard (1843–1917). *Courtesy of YCHC.*

Right: William L. Halsey (1836–1884). *Courtesy of YCHC.*

The competition that started at that point lasted for nine years. On one side was the old line (the Lake Keuka Navigation Co.) with its flagship, the *Urbana*, backed by Hammondsport business interests and, thanks to the Bath & Hammondsport Railroad, business interests in Corning and Elmira. On the other side was Halsey's company (the Crooked Lake Navigation Co.) with its flagship, the *Farley Holmes*, backed by Penn Yan business interests and, thanks to the North Central Railroad, business interests in Rochester and Buffalo. When William Halsey suddenly died in 1884, the company was taken over by his wife and T.O. Hamlin. They built one of the longest steamboats yet seen on the lake and named it the *William L. Halsey* when it was launched at Penn Yan in 1887. This allowed them, with the *Holmes* and the *Halsey*, to double-team the old line on the regular run between Penn Yan and Hammondsport. For nine years, there were lawsuits and injunctions, competition over docking rights and price slashing. Boats of the opposing lines raced each other to the docks to pick up the passengers first, resulting in a few collisions. The main beneficiary

The *Holmes*, flagship of the new line. *Courtesy of YCHC.*

The *Urbana*, flagship of the old line. *Courtesy of YCHC.*

of this competition was the public, as the price of an all-day ticket went from a dollar down to a dime.

With newer and more stylish boats, the new line held quite an advantage over the competition. However, both companies made huge profits as the flow of business increased dramatically on Keuka Lake. This attracted the attention of a New York City businessman Charles W. Drake, who was backed by other financiers. Drake started by buying the Bath & Hammondsport Railroad and the old line. He then set his sights on Mrs. Halsey, T.O. Hamlin and the new line. Rumors that Drake was going to have a steel-hulled boat built that would be the largest and finest on the lake, plus a purchase offer she couldn't refuse, caused Mrs. Halsey to sell her company and its boats to Drake in 1892, thus ending the last of the steamboat wars.

The steel-hulled boat that Drake built was the *Mary Bell*, which was launched at Hammondsport in May 1892. It cost $40,000 to build and was later described as the finest boat on any inland water in New York. It ended up being the last steamboat to carry passengers on Keuka Lake in 1922.

Charles Drake enjoyed his monopoly until 1904, when he sold all his holdings on the lake to the Erie Railroad. Being an astute businessman, he observed the general decline of steamboat business and was farsighted enough to see that gasoline and diesel engines would soon replace steam engines.

8

KEUKA LAKE'S BIGGEST FISH STORY

Perhaps the most famous photo in the history of Yates County was taken in 1873. It was widely distributed throughout the United States and Europe and helped to put Keuka Lake and Penn Yan on the map. The photo was of a boy and a fish.

The *Yates County Chronicle* of September 4, 1873, described the incident that led to the photo:

> *Dr. J.C. Mills has executed a photograph of Harry Morse, the little Trout Fisher, with the trout that tried to catch him. The picture sells by* [the] *hundreds. He also executed a fine stereograph representing the boy's mother as well as the boy and fish.*
>
> *A Wonderful Fish Story—The finny tribes have been the theme of many marvelous yarns, and frequently so incredible that a "fish story" has become the synonym for things more wonderful than veracious. The story we have to tell is marvelous and at the same time, as true as marvelous. The trout of our Lake are shy fish. It is not every slouch that entices them to grapple the hook. It is only the sagacious and wary angler that catches them on his line and lands them at will. It is true that they sometimes bite more greedily than at others, and perhaps that fact may help to account for the curious and apparently incredible yarn we are enabled to spin on the present occasion.*
>
> *On a pleasant sunny afternoon, August 27, 1873, Mrs. Ione Morse, widow of Myron Morse, and daughter of Reuben L. Corey of this village, with her little son Harry, seven years old, was quietly angling*

Harry Morse and his trout. *Courtesy of YCHC.*

> *for small fish near the shore at Brandy Bay on Lake Keuka. The mother was watching her line on one side of the skiff and the boy on the other. She was startled by a sudden scream from the lad and turning round, saw a large trout floundering in the bottom of the boat and the boy with a bloody face and terribly frightened. At the suggestion of someone on shore, she gave the fish a rap with an oar, which quieted him, then she pulled for land. It appeared that while the boy was leaning over the side of the boat with his face down near the water. The fish, which weighed about eight pounds, sprang from the water and struck his teeth into the boy's nose. Such was his momentum that, as the boy drew back from his approach, the fish fell over into the skiff and lost his life by his bold adventure. The boy's nose received a long and severe gash and the wound is yet very plainly visible. Such a thing as this was never heard of before in this quarter of the world and we are aware needs to be well vouched for to be believed. Of its truth there is not a shadow of a doubt. Although a wonderful fish story, it is not fishy in any dubious sense.*

Harry Morse carried that scar on his nose for the rest of his life and what a life he had. His uncle, Oscar Morse, was a well-respected steamboat captain on Keuka Lake and Harry, as a boy, went to work on the steamboats. As he grew older and more experienced, he rose from jobs on the crew to the more esteemed positions of pilot and captain. In 1892, at the age of twenty-six, he was hired as captain on the *Mary Bell*. The *Mary Bell*, with a steel hull and twin props, was a state-of-the-art steamboat. At 150 feet long, it was the biggest to ever sail on Keuka Lake. At a top speed of twenty miles per hour, it was also the fastest, able to make the trip from Penn Yan to Hammondsport in just over an hour. Described as "the finest boat on any inland waterway in New York," its interior had polished woodwork, fine upholstery and brass fittings. Because of its immense popularity, the *Mary Bell* often exceeded its stated capacity of 650 passengers. On one such occasion, Harry Morse had the boat off Bluff Point when a severe storm came up the lake. Rough water started to wash over the gunwales, and people onboard started to get very nervous. Someone shouted, "Don't worry! Harry is at the wheel!" One passenger who overheard that was a fellow from Mississippi named Booth Lowry. He was a poet who was in the area for an assembly at Keuka College. The storm blew over, and the *Mary Bell* made it's way to Penn Yan. By the time it got there, Lowrey had written this poem titled "Harry's at the Wheel":

Harry Morse and his mother (and his trout.) *Courtesy of YCHC.*

The crowds were surging fore and aft
The waves were rolling high,
The blackened clouds are marching forth,
And war is in the sky;
The Storm King hurls his sheeted bolts
Above and all around
And hill and valley echo back
The awe-inspiring sound.
But clouds may burst and winds may roar

And vessels rock and reel,
In triumph we will plow the waves,
For Harry's at the wheel.

See how the trees along the shore
Are bending humbly down;
See how the quivering meadows writhe
Beneath the storm cloud's frown;
See how the armored whitecaps rise
Like warships off the shore,
Then dash in fury each on each
And sink to rise no more.
Our gallant vessel quivers now
From topmost deck to keel,
But we'll defy the fiercest storm
While Harry's at the wheel.

Then frown, O Storm King, in your wrath
And hurl your bolts of fire;
Bring all your shadowed legions forth
To join a conflict dire.
The heaving bosom of the lake
In frenzy writhes beneath
And fiery daggers gleam above
From many a blackened sheath.
But we'll defy your howling blast
And furious thunder peal,
For we're aboard the Mary Bell
And Harry's at the wheel.[6]

Harry Morse didn't spend his whole life on the steamboats. He went west to Montana for a while to raise sheep in the late 1890s. He did that for eight years and then came back to Penn Yan. He tried the steamboats again for a while and then became interested in the new "moving picture shows" that were becoming popular. For five years, he leased and managed the Sampson Theater in Penn Yan. In 1921, Harry bought an old hotel on Elm Street named the Shearman House and transformed it into a movie theater called the Elmwood Theater, which opened to the public on May 27, 1921. The *Yates County Chronicle* of June 4, 1921, described the theater:

The *Mary Bell* (1892–1904), renamed the *Penn Yan* (1904–22). *Courtesy of YCHC.*

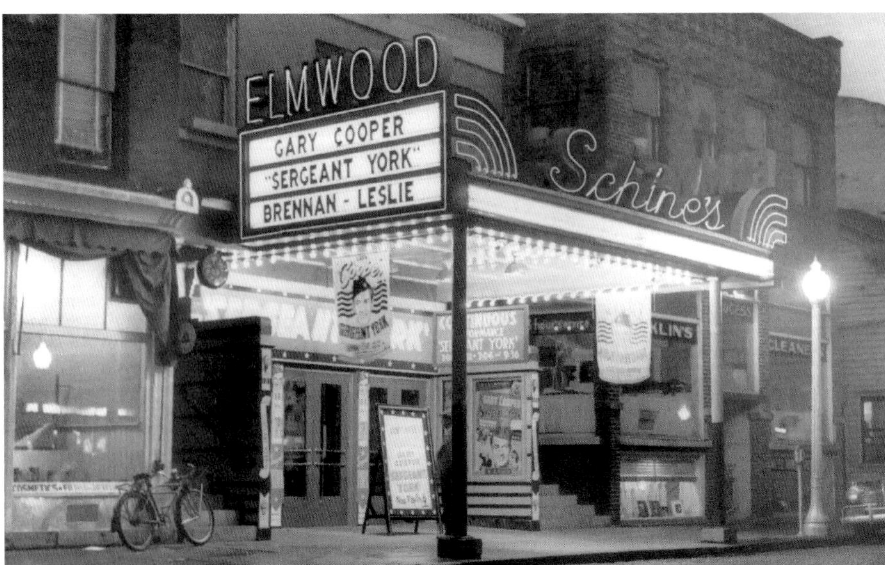

The Elmwood Theater in Penn Yan (1921–1971). The Village Office building is on that lot today. *Courtesy of YCHC.*

> *The Elmwood is a beautiful theater. Even those who had visited it frequently during the process of building, some of whom thought they knew just how it looked, were surprised when the lighting effects intensified the beauty of the decorations. The stage settings are very attractive and the effect was most pleasing…Everything about the theater creates an atmosphere of comfort. The woodwork in the foyer and lobbies is finished in French gray, harmonizing perfectly with the ivory and gold that's used with such good taste in the interior decorations. The introduction of an organ for use at all performances is a feature that is especially pleasing. On the opening night, the organ was played by Mr. Gifford of Rochester. In addition, there was a six-piece orchestra.*

Always with an eye on new technology (he was the first in Penn Yan to have a bicycle during the "wheeling craze" of the early 1890s), Morse invested in Vitaphone equipment in the late 1920s, which enabled his theater to show the new "talking movies." The first, *The Broadway Melody*, was shown on May 6, 1929. It ran for four days in Penn Yan to a packed house each time. The movie later became the first movie with sound to win the Academy Award for Best Picture. Morse quickly followed that up with two more sound movies: *The Terror* and *In Old Arizona*. Business was so good that summer that Harry Morse petitioned the village to allow movies to be shown on Sundays. It was put up for a special vote of Penn Yan residents and was passed 1,376 to 435. The silent movie era was over in Penn Yan.

Harry Morse died at his home on Keuka Street in Penn Yan in 1936 at the age of seventy. The Elmwood was sold later that year and became part of the Schine Brothers chain of theaters. With all that Harry Morse accomplished in his lifetime, he is most remembered for an eight-pound trout that he landed with his nose at the age of seven.

PART II

1900 TO 1920

9

THE NIGHT THE SHEPPARD OPERA HOUSE BURNED

People often ask about the Sheppard Opera House. Where was it? What happened to it? Many of us walk right past the old entrance to it in Penn Yan without being aware of it. There is a small alcove between the Lown Building and what today is the Yates County Arts Center. That alcove was the entranceway that led to the lobby of what was once called "one of the finest theaters in the Empire State." The theater itself was located in what today is the parking lot behind Lown's on Main Street in downtown Penn Yan. The Opera House was built during the winter of 1889–90 by the Penn Yan Opera House Company Limited, a state-chartered corporation whose president was Morris F. Sheppard. Two hundred shares of stock were sold to local businessmen at fifty dollars apiece to raise the money to begin construction. The architect was Leon Lempert of Rochester, who was renowned for his theater design throughout the Northeast. It had a main floor, a balcony, four balcony boxes and four loges, all of which sat about eight hundred people. The floors were beautifully carpeted, and the seats were "easy opera chairs." Opera glasses were available at each chair by depositing a dime in a slot. It was hailed as a credit to Penn Yan and as "the finest structure of the kind in this vicinity." Sometimes known as the Penn Yan Opera House, it was officially christened the Sheppard Opera House after the president of the company. It opened in March 1890 with two plays produced by the Madison Square Theater Company of New York City: the detective drama *Jim the Penman* and the comedy *The Private Secretary*. Tickets ranged from two dollars for the orchestra circle

The present-day location of the entrance to the Sheppard Opera House on Main Street in Penn Yan. *Author's collection.*

Opposite: Floor plan from the 1906–07 Penn Yan Village Directory. *Courtesy of YCHC.*

to fifty cents for the gallery at the back of the balcony. The first several performances were standing room only. From 1890 until 1907, the theater was the venue for various local productions, touring theater groups and musical concerts of all types. Over the years, it became known as the Yates Lyceum or the Lyceum Theater.

On the evening of March 18, 1907, just as the pianist was starting the overture preceding the first act of a touring musical production, someone entered the theater and hollered, "Fire! Fire!" After some initial confusion, ushers and other theater employees were able to oversee the evacuation of the theater by way of fire exits and fire escapes on both sides of the building. They were later given much credit for the fact that there was no loss of life. The cause of the fire was undetermined, but it was believed to have started under the hallway floor that led to the theater from Main Street. It quickly spread under the wooden floor throughout the entire building, which made it very difficult for fire fighters. "The fire swept through the Lyceum like a

Penn Yan Opera House

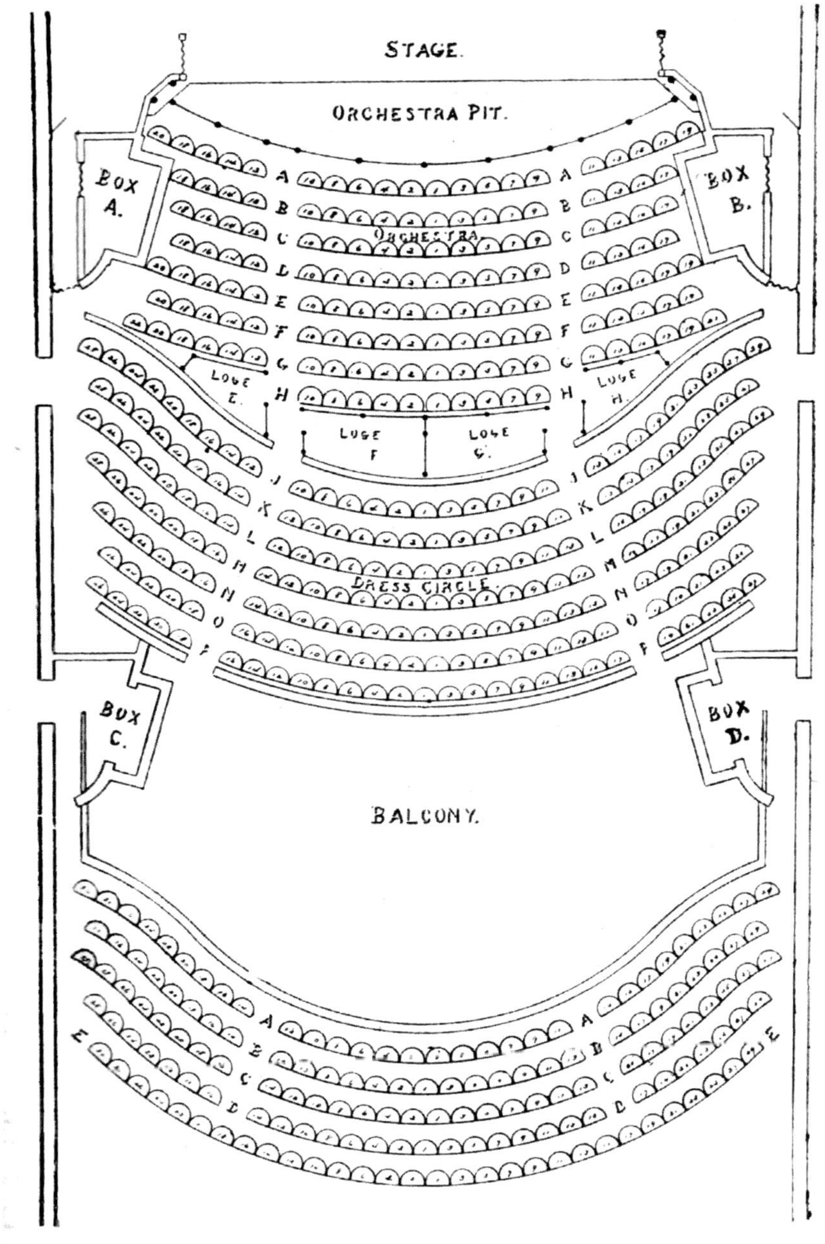

After the fire. *Courtesy of YCHC.*

huge wave and from every window tongues of flames were soon shooting forth," reported the *Yates County Chronicle*. Eight streams of water were trained on the theater by the fire department. Although the theater was doomed and the adjacent newspaper offices of the *Penn Yan Democrat* were ruined, firemen were given much credit for preventing the loss of that entire section of downtown Penn Yan. Other businesses and offices in the area experienced smoke and/or water damage, including Lown's Department Store, Cramer's five-and-ten-cent store and the Bell Telephone office. Total losses for all businesses that night were estimated at $20,000. It wasn't long before a stock company was organized to build a new theater in Penn Yan, which led to the construction of what eventually became known as the Sampson Theater on Elm Street.

The musical production that played that last night at the Lyceum Theater was *The Hottest Coon in Dixie*, a musical comedy presented by a company of black entertainers. Before anyone gets caught up in righteous indignation and political correctness over that title, it should be known that there was an entire genre of what were called "coon plays" and "coon songs" around the turn of the twentieth century. Formal Jim Crow–style segregation was becoming firmly entrenched, mainly in the South but also informally in other parts of the country, including the Northeast. These musical companies were a way that an entire generation of black entertainers (actors, musicians, comedians, singers, songwriters, playwrights, etc.) could find work—by entertaining mostly white audiences and catering to their racial stereotypes. The quality of the shows was several notches above that of black minstrel or vaudeville shows. Paul Laurence Dunbar, the noted poet, wrote dialogue for some of the plays. Scott Joplin's ragtime music was inspired by the "coon songs" used in these productions. The music also helped to lay the foundation of what later became known as "the blues."

The week after the fire destroyed the Lyceum Theater in Penn Yan, the editor of the *Yates County Chronicle*, using classic understatement, reported that "'The Hottest Coon in Dixie' proved to be a very hot number at the Yates Lyceum Monday night."

10

THE CANNON IN THE COURTHOUSE PARK

How silent are the guns today
While merry children 'round them play
How very little do they know
Their uses of the long ago.

Once, arbiters of human fate
They thundered forth a people's hate.
Today, but little more than toys
For happy, carefree girls and boys.

Again, as in the days of old,
Are raven locks and curls of gold.
Now shouts of glee with joy elate.
Then strife and tumult, death and hate.

Oh, can it be that cannon think
And with the past the present link?
Can they into the future peer
And con those days devoid of fear?

Postcard view of the Yates County Courthouse Park. *Courtesy of YCHC.*

When they at last have turned to rust
Their gunners all are naught but dust
Will mankind in that newer day
Still fight, or find a better way?

Poem by "A.F.R."
Chronicle-Express, *May 29, 1930*

As with many county seats around the country, Yates County has an impressive historic courthouse located in a beautiful park. County residents over the years have taken great pride in that. Part of what makes the setting impressive is the Soldiers and Sailors Monument that was formally dedicated on Memorial Day 1908.

The idea for a monument honoring those from Yates County who served in the Union cause during the Civil War was first introduced in 1890 by the Women's Relief Corps of Penn Yan, the auxiliary of the two local GAR (Grand Army of the Republic) posts. They wanted future generations to know that over 2,100 Yates County men, over 10 percent of the total county population, served in the War of the Rebellion. They hoped for a large monument in the park, but their fundraising campaign only succeeded in raising $600. As a result, they started thinking of just a plaque at the courthouse or perhaps a smaller monument in the cemetery. The idea was bandied about until finally, in February 1907, the GAR posts formed a committee to take over the project. On the committee were four county legislators, businessmen and others representing the community. Among the "others" was Frank Danes, the courthouse janitor, GAR member and survivor of Andersonville prison camp during the war.

As was the fashion throughout the country for these monuments, it was decided to acquire two surplus cannons from the war to flank the monument. Frank Danes had a nephew, Lieutenant Commander Frank H. Schofield of the navy, who, at the time, happened to be on shore duty, assigned to the Bureau of Ordnance in Washington, D.C. Danes wrote to his nephew:

> *Dear Frank,*
> *I guess you will get tired of my writing to you for the reason that I am always asking you to do something. Our committee thought the guns you marked were too large and it would be almost impossible for us to handle them as there is no one here that has any rig for that kind of business. We thought those light 12 pound Howitzers at the Washington Yard would do us. We have decided on a monument. It is to be 53 feet high and 14 feet square at the base. Write me what you think about them and if they are mounted; I take it they are, for it says "complete." We would like some projectiles, enough to make a mound of cannon balls. I don't think it would make much difference about the size. Frank, if there is anything you can give us any information on without compromising yourself, we would be glad to have it.*
>
> *Yours as ever,*
> *Uncle Frank*

What the committee wanted were the standard field pieces used by the army during the war, each of them weighing about eight hundred pounds. Schofield, being in naval ordnance, only had access to what the navy had in surplus. What he was able to acquire were nine-inch Dahlgren naval cannons, each weighing about eight thousand pounds.

One of the nine-inch Dahlgren naval cannons in the Courthouse Park, circa 1930s. *Courtesy of YCHC.*

Twenty-year-old Ralph Peckins of Benton was also in the navy, assigned to the USS *Indiana,* which was stationed at the Navy Yard in Philadelphia. In early September 1907, he had a letter published in the *Penn Yan Democrat*:

> *On August 23rd, the battleship* Indiana *sent a working party consisting of ten men and myself as petty officer in charge, down to the navy yard where the old wooden man-o-war,* Saratoga, *laid* [sic] *tugging lazily at her moorings. After boarding her, the working party was at once set to work releasing two old 9-inch cannon ("old war horses" as we called them) and hoisting them over the side onto the deck, but our work had only begun, for it was harder placing them on the flat car than taking them off the ship. Imagine us tugging away like Trojans on those "old war horses" when there was a 40-ton crane over our heads. I don't blame the government for working us like that, for if they used the crane it might wear out all the sooner. But you can imagine my surprise when I found out they were for the Penn Yan soldiers and sailors monument. If I had my say, I'd send about two score more cannons to Penn Yan to fortify the court house park.*

In addition to the two cannons, the committee was sent 224 cannonballs, each weighing seventy pounds. It all arrived around the time the above letter was published. The base of the monument was in place by then. There had been a ceremony on Memorial Day 1907, which included the laying of the cornerstone. In it were placed the names of the 2,109 men from the county who served during the war; rosters of all veteran's organizations in the county, including women's auxiliaries; an American flag; lists of county and village officials; copies of local newspapers; and a copy of Wolcott's Military History. The cornerstone alone weighed about six tons.

It was hoped that the shaft for the monument would be delivered in time for a complete dedication ceremony in late September. However, a piece of the stone had been spoiled by workers at the granite works in Barre, Vermont, so they put the main dedication off until Memorial Day 1908. On that day, with what was described as one of the largest crowds ever to gather in Yates County, the main speaker was Captain John F. Randolph. Randolph had been a private in the 126th New York Infantry and had risen through the ranks. In his speech, he paid special homage to the Keuka Rifles, the first company to leave Yates County for the war in May 1861. In a moving part of the speech, he asked the crowd to imagine the 2,109 men from the county marching past on Main Street. He "called out" several whom he knew personally: "There goes that rollicking dare-devil of a soldier, Garrett Ayres of Himrod of the 147th New York. It was not his to die the befitting death of a soldier, amid the rattle of musketry and clash of arms, but first to suffer a thousand deaths in a starving rebel prison pen." The monument cost a total of $6,000 and was partially financed by county taxpayers and partially by private donations.

Fast-forward three decades to 1938. With Hitler's armies marching into Austria and Czechoslovakia, Italian armies on the march in Africa and the Japanese advancing into the Chinese mainland, world events brought renewed determination to the American peace movement to stay out of any future war, which some saw as inevitable. A local movement began to pressure the county to remove the old cannons from the park. Those sentiments were reflected by letters to the editor of the *Chronicle-Express*. The following was written by retired Penn Yan businessman Theodore Hamlin in June 1938:

> *We approve of the suggestion to remove the cannon and balls from the Court House park. In addition to their being unsightly, they represent war instead of peace. They are also objectionable as they detract from the beauty of the soldier and sailors monument, a very fine artistic one and a credit to Penn Yan and Yates County.*

Another letter to the editor came from Louise Elsworth around the same time:

> *Last week a reminder was printed in the* Chronicle-Express *that just 30 years ago the Soldiers and Sailors Monument in the Court House park was unveiled. Would it not be a fitting time to restore the park to its attractive appearance at that time by removing the cannon, afterwards placed there, which detract so greatly from the dignity of the monument? These are a great eyesore to all of us who pass the park, which means all of us going through the village as well as to those of us living here who see the park daily. A more important consideration, however, is to remove from the children's background these grim reminders of conflict which will not be eradicated from the world until we stop bringing up the rising generation on the barbaric instruments of warfare.*

The peace movement in this country continued to grow as Europe was plunged into war by Hitler's invasion of Poland in September 1939. The sentiment to remove the old cannons from the park grew stronger as France fell to the Nazis in 1940 and the German air force attempted to bring Britain to its knees. However, those days of Charles Lindbergh, the America First Committee and "peace at any cost" yielded abruptly after Japan's attack on Pearl Harbor. For a while, at least, people forgot about the cannons in the Courthouse Park, but not for long.

One result of the rapid mobilization for war that occurred throughout 1942 was increased demand by the armaments industry for scrap metal. As part of the campaign called the National Emergency Scrap Metal Harvest, each state was given a quota that was broken down for each county. Yates County's quota was 850 tons to be collected by November 15. A letter to the editor of the *Chronicle-Express* published in early October 1942 noted:

> *The only war that meets my approval is a war of defense and we surely have reached that now! How can our city fathers better show their patriotism than by acceding to the urgent call from our government to give every bit of metal that can be spared to melt into armaments for defense of our loved country from slavery? When a neighboring city offers its enclosure of an iron fence about a public park to be used in defense of the Constitution handed down to us by our godly forefathers and of which we are so justly proud, shall we not imitate their example by removing from our otherwise pretty park the ugly implements of warfare—the cannons and balls that have so long disfigured it?*

One of the antitank guns presently in the park. *Author's collection.*

This time, the sentiment expressed in the letter reflected the feeling of most people in the county, and the county legislature released the cannons and cannonballs to be added to the drive. On October 15, the *Chronicle-Express* reported:

> *A good start on Yates County's quota of 850 tons of scrap metal to be collected the first week of November was made Saturday and the first of this week when the two Civil War naval cannons in the county court house park, Penn Yan, weighing 8,060 and 8,180 pounds respectively, were cut by a torch and loaded on a truck along with 8,690 pounds of cannon balls which for years formed the two display piles in the park near the cannon.*

The two guns that flank the Civil War monument these days are World War II–era fifty-seven-millimeter antitank guns that were made in 1942. They were donated to the county in the late 1940s by Rodney Pierce of Pierce Trucking, the forerunner of Penn Yan Express. It seems that rubber tires were still in short supply right after the war. Pierce acquired the two army surplus antitank guns, removed the tires and donated the guns to the county to replace the old Civil War cannons.

11

TITANIC REMEMBERED

Terrible Loss of Life at Sea
Largest Steamship in the World Goes Down after Ramming an Iceberg
Fear That 1,300 Passengers Perished
White Star Liner Titanic *Sank off Newfoundland Banks after Collision with Iceberg—Many New York Men of Vast Wealth Were on Board—Wireless Message Only News Received*
Yates County Chronicle, *April 17, 1912*

There is no need to retell the tragic story of the sinking of the RMS *Titanic*, especially after the 100th anniversary of the event was duly noted in April 2012. The story that does need to be told is how those headlines struck fear into the hearts of several residents of Yates County who knew people on board the ship. It was another week before the fate of friends and relatives on board the doomed luxury liner became known. There were three with Yates County connections with *Titanic*.

Howard B. Case, forty-nine years old, was among the missing and presumed dead. Born in Rochester in 1863, he lived in Yates County as a young boy. The April 24, 1912 issue of the *Yates County Chronicle* reported:

> *Howard Case of London, who lost his life on the* Titanic, *was known here. In 1864, '65, '66, his father, Charles Z. Case, preached in the Dresden Methodist Church and later in the Benton Center church. It was while he was a pastor of the latter church that he married a Miss Brown*

A night to remember: April 15, 1912. *Public domain.*

> *of Rochester and their first-born son was Howard. Howard was a great favorite in Benton, where he often visited after his mother moved to Rochester. The first money he ever earned after leaving school was selling the "Life of Moody" in that vicinity. He became an excellent businessman and after marrying, moved to Ashton, a suburb of London, where he represented the Vacuum Oil Company, a branch of the Standard Oil Company.*

He paid twenty-six pounds for a first-class cabin and boarded the ship at Southampton, England. He was on his way home to visit his family in Rochester. The following account comes from *The Sinking of the Titanic and Great Sea Disasters* by Logan Marshall, written in 1912:

> *Among the chivalrous young heroes of the* Titanic *disaster were Washington A. Roebling 2nd and Howard Case, London representative of the Vacuum Oil Company. Both were urged repeatedly to take places in lifeboats, but scorned the opportunity while working against time to save the women aboard the ill-fated ship. Both of these young men aided in*

the saving of Mrs. William T. Graham, wife of the President of the American Can Company, and Mrs. Graham's nineteen-year-old daughter, Margaret. Afterwards relating some of her experiences, Mrs. Graham said "Mr. Roebling came up and told us to get into the third lifeboat. Mr. Roebling and Mr. Case bustled our party of three into that boat in less time than it takes to tell it. They were both working hard to help the women and children. The boat was fairly crowded when we three were pushed into it and a few men jumped in at the last minute, but Mr. Roebling and Mr. Case stood at the rail and made no attempt to get into the boat. They shouted good-bye to us. What do you think Mr. Case did then? He just calmly lighted a cigarette and waved us good-bye with his hand. Mr. Roebling stood there too—I can see him now. I am sure they knew that the ship would go to the bottom, but both just stood there.

Margaret Welles Swift, forty-six years old, was put on a lifeboat and rescued. Born in Bath, New York, her maiden name was Margaret Barron, and as a young lady she spent her summers on Keuka Lake. She had many friends in Penn Yan who anxiously awaited news about her. A front-page article in the April 24 issue of the *Yates County Chronicle* ran under the headline "Mrs. Swift a Titanic Survivor." Widowed, she boarded the ship at Southampton and shared a first-class cabin with a friend, a female physician from New York City. They were on the last leg of an extended tour of Europe and were headed home. The *Chronicle* reprinted an interview that Mrs. Swift had with the *New York Evening Post*:

Mrs. Swift said she was taken off the Titanic *on the second lifeboat, in which there were twenty-four persons, including one sailor and three stewards. It was bitter cold and the women in her boat kept their blood in circulation by taking turns at the oars. "It was 11:45 pm by my watch," said Mrs. Swift, "when the ship struck the iceberg. I did not feel much shock, it sounded like a crash of glass. The ship seemed to strike the berg a glancing blow and the pieces of ice came through the portholes into the cabins. No one seemed to think the danger was very great and the stewards came around and said there was no danger. Some of the passengers went back to bed. I did too, but five minutes later, when the engines stopped, I became nervous and got up and dressed. It was thirty or forty minutes before we realized our danger. When the terrible moment came, the men acted like heroes. They gave way and assisted the women and children to places in the lifeboats. The stewards went around handing out and adjusting lifebelts on*

> *the women. When our boat was lowered, we were instructed to steer for the light of a fishing vessel. We missed it, however. It was 2:20 am according to my watch when the* Titanic *went down. We were about a mile away at the time. One of the ship's officers since told me that the* Titanic *broke in two before she went down.*

Mrs. Swift's lifeboat was rescued by the *Carpathia*, another Cunard ocean liner, in the early morning hours. When she returned to New York City, she sent a postcard to a friend in Penn Yan, Mrs. Charles W. Kimball. She mentioned that she was not injured and that she pulled an oar on the lifeboat for six hours without relief. She stated that "her early practice of rowing on Lake Keuka was of inestimable value to her in this crisis."

Delia Fallon, who was the sister of Mrs. Joseph (Nora) Mahan of Penn Yan and who also had many friends in the village, missed the boat. According to the article in the *Chronicle*:

> *Because they missed a train in Ireland, Miss Delia Fallon and sister, who arrived in Penn Yan Sunday, perhaps escaped death through their failure to board the* Titanic, *on which they expected to arrive in this country. Miss Fallon paid a visit to the old home in Ireland last summer. On her return this spring, she brought with her a younger sister and they wrote to Mrs. Mahan that they would sail on the* Titanic. *When the news of the catastrophe became public and the names of the survivors were sent from the* Carpathia, *the Fallon girls were not among the list of saved and consequently the assumption was that they had drowned. While they were being sorrowed for here, they were sailing to America in another vessel, all unconscious of the grief that was being endured by their relatives here. Reaching New York, they sent a message to Penn Yan that brought joy where gloom reigned.*

12
YATES COUNTY AND WOMEN'S SUFFRAGE

Rosalie Jones was a suffragette from Long Island. In 1912 and 1913, she organized a series of "suffrage hikes" around the Northeast to drum up support for getting women the right to vote. The following story comes from the June 20, 1913 issue of the *Yates County Chronicle* and describes a humorous scene at the Four Corners in Penn Yan:

> *Suffragettes on the Corner—Two members of the Rosalie Jones band of suffragettes were in Penn Yan Wednesday night and held a meeting near the corner of Main and Elm Street. At the hotel where they put up, one registered as "a militant from England" and the other as "a plain suffragette from New York." The "militant" suffragette who came here was a fraud. She and her companion selected a spot on Bordwell's corner where they intended to hold forth and then went for supper. When they returned, a man had taken possession of the place and was offering a variety of articles for sale. There was a chance for Miss Suffragette to show her militancy. But instead of shoving Mr. Man from the vantage point previously chosen, she meekly led her partner to the opposite side of the street and climbed up on a little box about a foot square to begin her talk. Just as she was ready, another man with a popcorn and peanut wagon came along and wheeled it right up by the side of the Misses Suffragette and again the militant one failed to show any sign of fight or even of anger. In fact, the two suffragettes seemed to enjoy the situation just as much as did the young men who gathered around. While Miss Suffragette was talking, many women*

> *passed by on the opposite side of the street but none gathered around the crusader or offered the least encouragement. The tooting of automobile horns, the clanging of street car bells, or the occasional joshing by somebody in the charmed circle did not ruffle the temper of Miss Suffragette in the least, so we know she was a fraud. No militant suffragette from England would stand for any such treatment without starting something.*

New York State women did not have to wait for the ratification of the Nineteenth Amendment to the U.S. Constitution in 1919. An amendment to the New York State constitution extended the vote to women two years earlier. In 1917, New York became the first eastern state to grant full voting rights to women, the twelfth state overall. However, that didn't happen without a struggle.

It was natural that Yates County would play an active role in that struggle. In 1855, just eight years after the first women's rights convention in nearby Seneca Falls, a similar convention was held on Main Street in Penn Yan. The main speaker at that convention was Susan B. Anthony of Rochester, who clearly stated that full voting rights for women was a primary goal of their movement. The issue slowly picked up momentum during the next half a century. It was the Progressive movement of the early 1900s that intensified the energy of those pushing for women's suffrage in the county and the state. New Yorker Theodore Roosevelt had full voting rights for women on the party platform for his failed third-party bid in the 1912 presidential election. That election resulted in another progressive, Woodrow Wilson, taking over the presidency, and suffragists around the country were further encouraged. Wilson, however, had other priorities, so the women's movement intensified its efforts.

In the summer of 1913, it was announced that the question of women's suffrage would be put before the (male) voters of New York as a referendum in November 1915. In Penn Yan, a group was organized in August 1913 called the Political Equality Club. A similar group was formed in Dundee. They both became part of the statewide suffrage movement with a focus on the November 1915 referendum. Local suffragette leaders included Mrs. Charles Day, Mrs. Wendell Bush, Mrs. F.G. Merson, Ada Chapman, Eva Wise, Elizabeth Cramer, Ursala Swarts and Louise Sheppard. For two years, these groups held parlor meetings in private homes (called "pink teas"), rallies in churches, outdoor rallies and automobile parades. They distributed literature and brought in the best speakers from the statewide organization. They took their cause to every village, hamlet and four corners in Yates

County. At a street rally in Penn Yan on Memorial Day 1915, the *Yates County Chronicle* reported:

> *Great interest was shown by the crowds that stopped to hear. Especially was this so when one old veteran declared that if women were given the vote, they should shoulder the musket and go to war. He was answered with much warmth by a comrade, who said his mother and sister had done all the work on a hundred and fifty acre farm while he was at war and that he considered their share of the work harder than his own.*

As the 1915 referendum approached, the women gained important male allies. In September of that year, the Yates County Men's League for Women's Suffrage was formed with members from every town in the county. Their organization was composed of public officials, clergymen and business leaders. They held their own rallies to sway the male vote.

When the votes were counted in November, the women's suffrage referendum went down to a crushing defeat statewide. In Yates County, 2,687 men voted No and only 1,396 voted Yes. The turnout was considered quite low as many men were indifferent to the issue. However, the spirit of the suffrage movement was not crushed. If anything, the leaders of the organization became more determined. The leader of the local movement, Mrs. Frankie G. Merson of Keuka Park, wrote in a letter to the editor of the *Chronicle* "the women of our county have found themselves and will enjoy a fuller fellowship in future efforts than would have been possible before this campaign." The statewide organization held its convention in Albany a year later. The state chair, Mrs. Vira Whitehouse, told the convention: "We failed because we worked like amateurs; we worked for suffrage when our work did not interfere with pleasures, or when our duty to suffrage did not interfere with other duties." Another speaker said, "No more pink teas, no more parlor meetings and abstract lectures for the suffrage cause. We are in the home stretch and we no longer need debates and historical summaries. We are a political organization and we are going to give straight votes-for-women appeals from this time on."[7]

With that, they focused on getting the referendum on the ballot again in 1917 but determined to work harder for a different result. The white, elbow-length gloves were off.

In preparation for the 1917 campaign, the groups in Yates County that favored women's suffrage combined into the Yates County branch of the New York State Women's Suffrage Party. The head of the county organization was Florence Upson of Dundee, and Mrs. Frankie Merson, a professor at Keuka College, was an organizer and liaison to the statewide group. Once again, the group took the movement to every corner of Yates County, holding rallies, bringing in speakers and getting women's signatures on petitions that simply said, "I, the undersigned, believe that the vote should be given to the women of New York State." By the summer of 1917, there were over 3,600 signatures on those petitions. That was all part of a statewide campaign to enroll one million women in the movement.

Events in 1917 seemed to favor the extension of the vote to women. In April, President Wilson asked Congress for a declaration of war against Germany, and the United States joined England and France in the Great War. There was a lot of talk about making the world safe for democracy and protecting the rights of free people everywhere. As the country mobilized for war that summer, women were asked to fill in for the men in factories and out on the farm. Women were being asked to join the Red Cross, get involved in food conservation, join Liberty Loan drives and Women's War Relief. Suffrage movements in England and Canada were on the brink of realizing their goals.

In late August, Yates County delegates took the 3,600 signatures on their petitions to the statewide conference in Saratoga, where, combined with the other counties, there was a grand total of over one million women on record wanting the vote. Yates County was recognized at the conference for having over 50 percent of its women enrolled. According to Mrs. Merson, "The delegates came back to Yates County knowing more surely than ever that the glorious vision of a world democracy that is rising before every people adds to our efforts for a complete democracy in the United States. To quote the dying words of Susan B. Anthony 'Failure is impossible.'" That September, the local chapter set up a "rest tent" at the Yates County Fair in Penn Yan where members of the movement handed out lemonade, literature and buttons and had notable speakers. They did the same at the Dundee Fair in October. One speaker pointed out that eight million women in other states were able to vote in presidential elections.

In late October, just one week before election day, Yates County's petitions for women's suffrage were pasted onto five placards and were taken by local delegates to New York City for a massive parade of suffragettes down Fifth Avenue. Women carried petitions from across New York State with well over one million signatures on them. It turned out to be the last parade for women's suffrage in New York. With the support of the governor behind the resolution, as well as the majority of the legislature, passage of the referendum

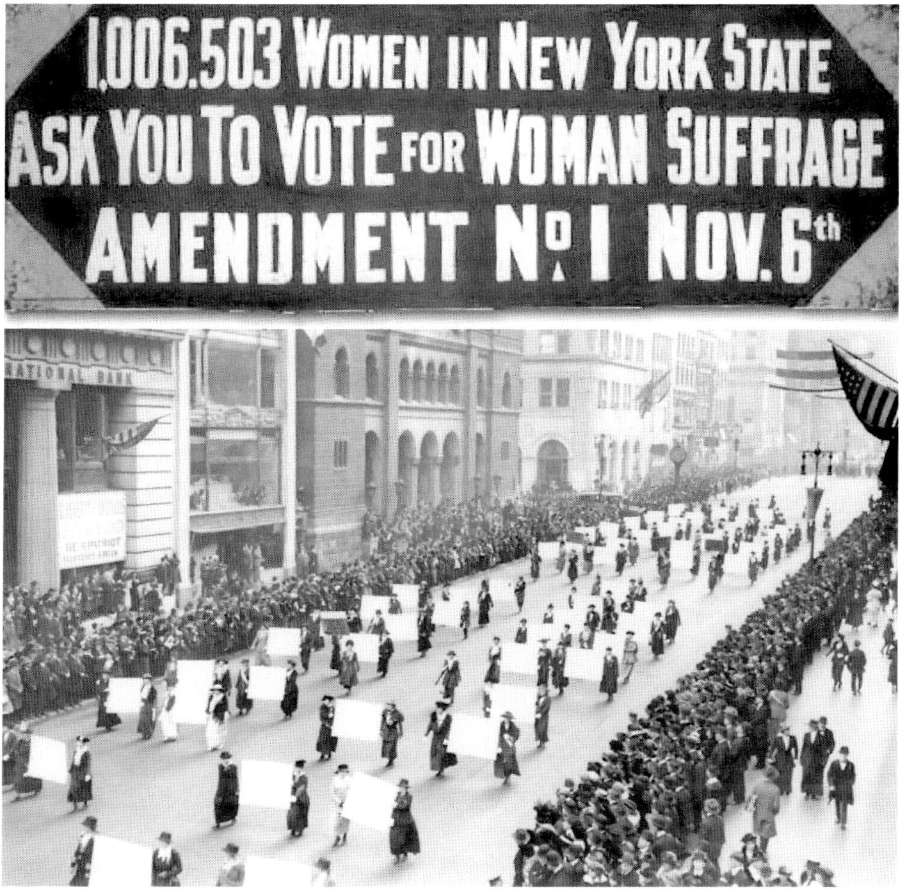

Suffrage parade in New York City in October 1917. *Public domain.*

on the ballot was considered a certainty. The county's petitions were brought back to Penn Yan and placed in the window of Lynch Brothers Department Store on Main Street for the few days before the election. As the editor of the *Yates County Chronicle* stated in endorsing passage of the referendum, "The women understand they are struggling against deep-rooted prejudice in so conservative a state as New York, but they look forward to victory." Mrs. Merson, in a letter to the newspaper, wrote, "Ninety-five percent of the voters of Yates County will believe in women suffrage before the war is over. We only ask you to think ahead now, before November 6th. Time, effort, prayers have gone into this campaign. There are scores of women in Yates County who have given all their leisure for patriotic and suffrage work."

On election day, the referendum on the ballot favoring full voting rights for women passed statewide by a wide margin, and the women of New York did not have to wait for the federal constitutional amendment to be ratified after the war. However, in Yates County the referendum was overwhelmingly defeated. The *Chronicle* reported, "The vote for women's suffrage in Yates County at last week's election resulted in 1,425 votes for the amendment and 2,242 against. In 1915, the vote stood 1,396 for and 2,687 against the proposition. In no district in the county in 1915 or 1917 did the women receive a majority of he votes. The town of Italy came the nearest, there being 49 votes for and 59 against the proposition this year." It was the largest margin of defeat in any county in the state. Those who opposed suffrage had no organization and mounted no campaign.

Certainly disappointed over the local results, the members of the Yates County branch of the New York State Women's Suffrage Party gathered at the Benham Hotel in Penn Yan that December to celebrate the statewide victory in a "Women's Citizen's Luncheon." County leader Florence Upson was one of eight hundred leaders who attended the victory banquet at the Biltmore Hotel in New York City and gave a full report on that. They had lost the local battle against ignorance and apathy but took great satisfaction in winning the ultimate goal: full voting rights.

Those five placards with the 3,600 signatures of women in the county who wanted the vote were presented to the Yates County Genealogical & Historical Society in 1940 by Mrs. Alexander R. Thompson of Penn Yan, who was the treasurer of the county branch of the state suffrage party. They have been a proud part of our collection and have been displayed several times over the years. Is your grandmother or great-grandmother on there? Go into the Yates County History Center (Underwood Museum) and see!

13

SUSAN MILLER DORSEY (1857–1946)

Yates County has produced a few female "pioneers" over the years. The first one to come to mind would be Jemima Wilkinson, the "Publick Universal Friend," who, although not a native of the area, was critical to the early development of what eventually became Yates County. She was the first American-born woman to found a religious group. Lesser known, but no less significant, was Susan Miller Dorsey. She was a native of Yates County who went on to become the first female superintendent of a major metropolitan school district in the country in Los Angeles, California.

Susan Miller was born just outside the village of Penn Yan in 1857. Her parents were James and Hannah Benedict Miller and the family farm was in the Town of Jerusalem near where Sherman Hollow Road branches off from County House Road. An excellent student, she set her goal very early to be a teacher. She graduated from Penn Yan Academy in 1873 at the age of sixteen and immediately went off to Vassar College in Poughkeepsie. She graduated from there four years later having majored in Greek, Latin, history and English and having earned a Phi Beta Kappa key. Susan Miller immediately landed her first job, teaching the classics at Wilson College, a women's school in Chambersburg, Pennsylvania. She taught there for just one year when a death on the faculty at Vassar caused the administration there to locate Susan and entice her back to Vassar as an instructor in Greek and Latin. She taught at her alma mater for three years. During that time, she married Patrick Dorsey, another Yates County native, who was starting his career as a Baptist minster. In 1884, Reverend Dorsey received a call

Susan Miller Dorsey. *Courtesy of YCHC.*

to minister to a congregation in Los Angeles (at that time a village of less than twelve thousand people) and the newly married couple went west. The Dorseys had a son born out there, but the marriage did not work out. Abandoned by her husband and their son in the early 1890s, Susan Dorsey worked for a while as a social worker and then went to work teaching Latin in the only high school in Los Angeles in 1896. She quickly rose through the ranks from teacher to department head to assistant principal. In 1913, she was appointed assistant superintendent of the Los Angeles schools, and in 1920, at the age of sixty-three, she was chosen to be superintendent, a post that she initially declined; however, the board of education refused to consider that, and she eventually accepted.

During the nine years she was superintendent, the population of Los Angeles more than doubled, which was reflected in the student population of the school district. It was the fastest-growing school district in the world in the 1920s. Dealing with this record growth was Mrs. Dorsey's biggest challenge. In 1927, she said, "In seven years our attendance has increased from 100,000 to 200,000. No school system and no city in the world has had to cope with such a problem. One year ago we had one hundred buildings under construction at the same time. Today we are caught up with our building program but this year the school attendance has increased 14,000 again."[8] When she retired in 1929, she ran a school district with over four hundred buildings and a yearly budget of over $30 million. Aside from dealing with the rapid growth of the district, Mrs. Dorsey was credited with developing their kindergarten program, establishing an Americanization program for foreign-born students and found ways for the district to adapt to the needs of handicapped students and those with special reading difficulties. She oversaw the development of courses for teaching California history and started a vocational training program.

What is most striking to learn about Susan Miller Dorsey (especially for this writer, a retired career educator) was the love and respect that the people of her district had for her. When she announced her retirement in 1928 at the age of seventy-two, the teachers of Los Angeles raised the money to commission a professional artist, John Hubbard Rich of Hollywood, to paint her portrait. A photo of that portrait is included in this chapter. For the unveiling of the portrait, a special ceremony was held at the Shrine Auditorium in Los Angeles in January 1929 and attended by hundreds. The *Los Angeles School Journal* reported, "A cap and gown processional composed of college professors, leading educators, and outstanding public officials will precede the ceremonies." The governor of California and the mayor of Los Angeles both spoke, and there was a major address by the dean of the University of California. The portrait was presented to the county of Los Angeles to be displayed in its art gallery. In 1937, a new high school was opened in the city and named Susan Miller Dorsey High School, the only time a school in L.A. was named after a living person. At that time, the portrait was moved to the library of the school and hung there for thirty years. Over the years, Mrs. Dorsey was awarded honorary degrees by Vassar College (probably a Doctorate of Arts), Pomona College, Occidental College, the University of Southern California and the University of California. Susan Miller Dorsey High School is still going strong in south Los Angeles. There is a dormitory named in her honor at Scripps College in Claremont, California, where she once sat on the board of trustees, and there is still a scholarship fund in her name at Vassar. She died in Los Angeles in 1946 at the age of eighty-nine.

There is an interesting story involving her portrait. Janet Colman, a student at Susan Miller Dorsey High School in the early 1960s, was impressed by the portrait and was motivated to learn more about the woman in it. What she learned partially influenced her decision to go into teaching as a profession. After college in 1970, Mrs. Colman came back to teach at Dorsey High and noticed that the portrait was missing. She became obsessed with locating the portrait and eventually learned that when the high school library was being painted in the late 1960s, it was returned to Los Angeles County. The portrait was then deaccessioned and put on sale in the early 1980s. By chance, in 1985 Mrs. Colman learned that it was hanging in a private home, having been bought by a man who wanted a portrait done by John Hubbard Rich. He had no idea who the woman in the painting was. Janet Colman went to the man's home and asked if she could purchase the portrait. He eventually got back to her with an asking price of $25,000, and the price floored her. Her husband, knowing how much his wife valued the portrait, worked out a deal with the man who owned it. Janet and her husband run a business in Los Angeles that collects and sells old movie posters. He offered $25,000 worth of collectable movie posters for the portrait of Susan Miller Dorsey. The deal was made, and Susan Miller Dorsey's portrait has hung in the Colman's living room in Los Angeles since 1986 and will eventually be given back to the high school.

PART III

1920 TO 1940

14

PAUL GARRETT

Yates County's Wine Tycoon

I drive past the old Garrett Wine building near the Liberty Street Bridge in Penn Yan almost every day. Workmen have renovated the exterior in the past few years, and it probably looks better now than it ever did. Most people aren't aware that that old building was once a major part of a national wine empire that included many thousands of acres of vineyards and seventeen processing plants in six states. It was all owned and operated by Paul Garrett, who spent summers on Keuka Lake between 1913 and his death in 1940. A local writer, Emerson Klees, recently published a book on Garrett and his wine empire titled *Paul Garrett: Dean of American Winemakers*, which I read for background on this chapter. I also scoured through files at the Yates County History Center and spent hours reading local newspapers from the time period that Garrett was in the area. I visited the Greyton H. Taylor Wine Museum in Hammondsport and met with museum director Paul Sprague to get his input. I was also in contact with John Barden of Rochester, a great grandson of Paul Garrett, who gave me feedback on and provided me with the photos of the Garrett family. I appreciate all the assistance.

Paul Garrett was already "the Dean of American Winemakers" when he moved to Yates County. He went to work for his family's winery in North Carolina in 1877 at the age of fourteen and eventually became the company's top salesman. After his father and uncle died, Paul worked for the new owners but eventually had a falling out with them over his sales commissions. Around 1900, he set off on his own and founded Garrett & Co. His bestselling wine, Virginia Dare, with the distinctive taste of scuppernong

The Old Garrett Wine Building in Penn Yan. *Author's collection.*

grapes prevalent in North Carolina, became the bestselling wine in America as a result of Garrett's marketing techniques. When North Carolina enacted statewide prohibition in 1908, Garrett moved his company's headquarters to Norfolk, Virginia. When it became clear that Virginia would soon do the same, Garrett moved his headquarters to New York in 1912. He was familiar with the Penn Yan area, having bought grapes from area farmers for several years, and he even owned a small processing plant in Penn Yan that pressed grapes into juice to be shipped to his winery in Virginia. In April 1913, he leased the building along the outlet on Liberty Street from William Wise, the "Grape King." Wise had used it as a warehouse to store fruit baskets. A company called Superior Tack & Nail was also using part of the building. Garrett converted the entire building over to pressing grapes. The juice was sent to his plant in Virginia in specially made railroad tank cars, where it was made into wine. (Through a quirk in Virginia's prohibition law, wine could still be manufactured there; it just couldn't be sold.) In 1914, Garrett bought land on the end of Bluff Point and had a beautiful summer home and boathouse built in 1917. At the same time, he bought up farmland around the county for vineyards and made arrangements with area farmers to buy their grapes. At his peak, he owned nearly four thousand acres of vineyards in the Keuka Lake area.

United States' involvement in the Great War in Europe in 1917 created a political climate that encouraged passage of national Prohibition, a movement that had been building for decades. The Eighteenth Amendment was passed by Congress in December 1917 and sent to the states for ratification. By January 1919, the required number of states had ratified the amendment, and it was scheduled to take effect in January 1920. During that year, the specifics of the enforcement of the amendment were written into the Volstead Act. The bill was largely written by the Anti-Saloon League, the main Prohibition lobby. Paul Garrett, representing agricultural interests (grape farmers), worked to have certain exceptions included. Among them was the provision that nonintoxicating cider and fruit juice could be made in the home for domestic use. That exception became a key factor in allowing Garrett & Co. to survive Prohibition.

Garrett firmly believed that the "Noble Experiment" would not last long, and he had plans underway that would allow his company to prosper even with Prohibition. He utilized the local press to reassure local farmers, telling them that he would construct a new plant in Penn Yan in order to make grape preserves and that he would need to buy five thousand tons of grapes a year from them. The *Yates County Chronicle* added, "With this new demand for Lake Keuka's luscious fruit and the increased call for table grapes which there is every reason to expect, the grape grower need have few sleepless nights." In the months before Prohibition took effect, Garrett rented the White Top Winery near Gibson's Landing on Keuka Lake to step up wine production. He also bought two large boats, the *City of Rochester* and the *City of Elmira*, to ship grapes on the lake to his plants in Penn Yan, Hammondsport and Gibson's Landing. By the time Prohibition took effect, Garrett & Co. owned seventeen processing plants in six states (North Carolina, Virginia, Ohio, Missouri, New York and California) that produced about 10 million gallons of wine a year.

Another important move that Paul Garrett made in 1919 was to buy a plant in Brooklyn and hire a chemist by the name of Bernard Smith. Company lawyers saw a loophole in Prohibition that would allow wine to be manufactured and transported as long as it was not sold as an alcoholic beverage. Garrett's plan was to ship his wine to the plant in Brooklyn, where, through "a secret process" developed by Smith, the alcohol was extracted. The alcohol-free wine was sold under the name of Virginia Dare. Company advertising claimed,

"All the flavor and aroma that have been a joy to connoisseurs for nearly a century. All the wholesome goodness of the health-giving grapes discovered by Sir Walter Raleigh. All the thirst-satisfying qualities of the famous beverage. Nothing missing but the alcohol and you won't miss that in the new delight of this fine wine." Well, people did miss the alcohol, and the alcohol-free wine never caught on. What did catch on was the extracted alcohol, which was turned into flavoring extracts—peppermint, vanilla, orange, lemon, coffee, etc.—and sold to the food industry and consumers under the name Virginia Dare Extract Co., a company that is still in business. Garrett sold the extract company in the mid-1920s to the family that still operates it today under the same brand name.

In the last years of Prohibition, Garrett focused on selling cans of grape concentrate with packets of yeast and instructions on how to make wine in the home. As mentioned earlier, the Volstead Act allowed nonintoxicating cider and fruit juice to be made in the home for domestic use (thanks to Garrett). By the late 1920s, the IRS had determined that the maximum amount that could be made was two hundred gallons a year, and federal court cases had basically rendered the term "nonintoxicating" meaningless. Garrett & Co. combined with a few influential California wineries into Fruit Industries Inc. and sold the product under the name of Vine-Glo. The federal government took Fruit Industries into court over that, but the wineries won the case in 1928.

In the 1920s and 1930s, the Garrett family split their time between homes in New Rochelle, New York, and Santa Barbara, California, with occasional visits to their holdings in Virginia and other parts of the country. However, their summers each year were spent on Keuka Lake. Paul Garrett expanded his land base on Bluff Point, eventually acquiring 1,200 acres, including the entire end of the bluff. He also had large vineyards in Milo and Wayne near Keuka Lake. He became a major player in local business, politics and the summer social scene. He was commodore of the Keuka Lake Yacht Club for several years, and his son, Charles, and daughter, Evelyn, raced both sailboats and power boats in competition. For a while, Paul Garrett had one of the fastest boats on the lake, the thirty-three-foot *Virginia Dare*, which unfortunately caught fire in their boat house in 1927. It was immediately replaced with an identical Gar Wood boat, which was named *Virginia Dare II*.

In 1923 Robert Moses, backed by Governor Al Smith, proposed a major expansion of New York's state park system. Garrett, realizing what a state park could do for the economy of this area, bought the Wagener Mansion on top of Bluff Point and developed a plan to create a state park, using the

Paul Garrett (1863–1940). *Photo provided by John Barden, Garrett family collection.*

mansion as the park's administration building. In August of that year, he held a big picnic there to get local leaders on board with the idea. The next year, he sold one hundred acres to the State of New York for the purpose of establishing the park. The one hundred acres stretched from the mansion down to the Keuka shoreline, where there was 1,225 feet of lake frontage. The plan called for a large resort hotel, two golf courses, an airfield and rest camp for aviators, tennis courts, baseball fields, boulevards, a large picnic pavilion, automobile tourist camps and an extension of the trolley line from Penn Yan and Branchport. He got Penn Yan's Walter Tower squarely behind the project. Tower was a realtor, president of the Penn Yan Chamber of

Commerce and on the board of the newly formed Finger Lakes Association. In August 1923, the leaders of the plan to establish a state park held a huge picnic and Virginia barbecue on the lawn of the Wagener Mansion. Over six hundred state and local leaders attended for an afternoon and evening of good food, boat rides, baseball games and tours of the grounds of the potential state park. A highlight was described by the local newspapers:

> *And out of the skies over the sapphire expanse of waters came a government airplane, the first to use the plateau of Bluff Point as a landing field to demonstrate the federal government's interest in developing the point 1,350 feet above sea level as an official landing field. The plane was sent for the occasion from Mitchell Field under government orders with the aviator, Lieut. E.H. Barksdale, one of the aces of the flying service, as a guest at the barbecue.*

That was followed by speeches promoting the park concept on the front lawn of the mansion with that beautiful view of the lake in the background. Needless to say, the guests left Bluff Point that evening with a full head of steam to see the park became reality. In December of that year, the State of New York agreed to buy the one hundred acres for $15,000, and the Bluff Point State Park looked like a sure thing.

While the plan was awaiting state funding, Garrett proceeded to further develop the end of Bluff Point. He proposed that the county build a road from Keuka Park along the Keuka shoreline and around the end of the bluff. He described it as "14 miles of scenic splendor." The county didn't go for the idea, so Garrett bought a steam shovel and hired a contractor to build a road from the Wagener Mansion down to the end of the bluff and eventually to the Keuka shoreline a mile north of his summer home. That roadway still exists. He even proposed to change the name of Keuka Lake to Guyanoga Lake. He thought that too many people from outside the area were confusing it with Cayuga Lake. Business interests in Seneca Falls were going through the process of creating Cayuga Lake State Park at that same time. Garrett's idea created a wave of protest from the community and one critic wrote a poem for the *Penn Yan Democrat*: "Oh Keuka, Fair Keuka / Thy fame they are trying to hide / By taking away thy fair name / To which we point with pride." The name change never caught on with the public; the state park didn't catch on with the state legislature, which never provided the funding for it; and the aviator's rest camp never caught on with the U.S. Air Service.

The Garrett summer home on Bluff Point at Keuka Lake. *Author's collection.*

Paul Garrett and his family at Keuka Lake in the summer of 1925. *Photo provided by John Barden, Garrett family collection.*

Left with few options for his land on Bluff Point, in 1929 Garrett agreed to sell 1,200 acres to Francis E. Getchell of Pittsburg, who represented "outside financial interests." Like Garrett, Getchell was a man who thought big and saw great potential on Bluff Point. His plan, which was an expansion of Garrett's, was to secure options on 6,000 acres of Bluff Point, on a line from Keuka Park to Branchport, and turn it into "a millionaire's paradise." Getchell formed a holding company, Bluff Point–Lake Keuka Management Inc., with capital of $10 million that would sell shares of stock. The company would pump between $25 and $50 million into Bluff Point. The centerpiece was to be a one-thousand-room hotel that would cost $4.5 million. An airport was to be constructed, along with a bank and "two or three of the sportiest golf courses in America, a game preserve, bathing casino, yacht club, and summer homes," according to the *Chronicle-Express* of September 26, 1929. Getchell said:

> *Such a plan may seem visionary to many but in the modern age of rapid transportation by road and air, people in a score of cities in the Eastern United States would welcome a resort with the natural wonders possessed by Bluff Point and Lake Keuka. With an adequate airport located on the upper portion of the bluff which towers some 800 feet above the level of the lake, many businessmen would fly back and forth from the bluff to do their business in a distant city.*

Several concrete steps were taken toward making all that a reality. Options to buy involving over sixty property owners were acquired on five thousand of the six thousand acres on Bluff Point. A house was purchased on East Elm Street in Penn Yan to serve as corporate headquarters, and Getchell even bought Paul Garrett's speedboat *Coquette* to ferry prospective clients from Penn Yan to the end of the bluff. The holding company was formed in Delaware in September 1929, a board of directors was appointed and a president was chosen (a Detroit financier). Penn Yan realtor Walter Tower and the chamber of commerce promoted the development locally.

Just as things were falling into place for Getchell and the Bluff Point project, he was arrested in Rochester on a warrant from Pennsylvania as a fugitive from justice. He was wanted on a charge of conspiracy to defraud for a land deal in Bucks County outside Philadelphia. Getchell proclaimed his innocence and fought extradition to Pennsylvania. He was extradited and taken to Philadelphia, where he spent fourteen days in jail before standing trial. Locally, people were assured by Walter Tower and the chamber of commerce that this had nothing to do with the Bluff Point project and that no money had yet been taken out of Yates County. Just before Christmas 1929, Getchell was acquitted by a jury based on a lack of evidence. He claimed that he was framed by business competitors. He wrote a major letter to local newspapers explaining his side of the case and trying to reassure property owners and potential investors. It was to no avail; his credibility was shattered. Getchell's arrest and the stock market crash that October combined to create a mood of economic and ethical uncertainty that doomed the project to failure.

With the option off his 1,200 acres on Bluff Point, Paul Garrett formed his own holding company to oversee any future development of the land. He had been distracted by the rapidly worsening of the health of his only son, Charles. Paul Garrett intended for his son to take over his business empire, but Charles suffered for years with tuberculosis. He died in Tucson, Arizona, in January 1930. His last words to his mother were, "Don't leave me out here. Take me home to Bluff Point, take me home." His remains were put in a mausoleum in Los Angeles while his father made plans for "the Little Chapel on the Mount" on Bluff Point. The May 22, 1930 edition of the *Chronicle-Express* reported, "'Mr. Garrett Plans Chapel on Bluff Point Property'—Mr. Garrett is very much impressed by the Spanish type of architecture which makes the beautiful Kirk of the Heather, near Los Angeles, where the body of his late son Charles is reposing. It is possible that this small edifice will be practically duplicated here, being used by the Garrett family for worship and interment." Construction was started that summer, and the chapel was dedicated in July 1931. Charles's body was brought back from California and buried in the crypt, as were the remains of three other children of Paul Garrett's who had died in infancy.

When Prohibition ended in December 1933, with his wine making facilities basically intact, Garrett was ready to resume the sale of Virginia Dare wine. The problem was the shortage of scuppernong grapes that gave the wine its distinctive flavor. Southern farmers had shifted their land over to other crops during the 1920s. Garrett blended in other varieties of grapes, but he could not recapture the taste that Virginia Dare wine had in previous years, and its popularity declined. Throughout the 1930s, Garrett promoted the use of different varieties of grapes for wines and became the major spokesman for American-made wines. He wrote several pamphlets on the topic, and when the Liberty League used French wine at a dinner to honor former New York governor Al Smith in 1936, Garrett protested loudly. In the late 1930s, he unsuccessfully petitioned for federal legislation to have wine classified as a food product. He felt that by removing the liquor tax from wine, thus lowering the price, U.S. wine could compete favorably with foreign wine. Early in 1940, Paul Garrett caught pneumonia and died in New York City at the age of seventy-six. His remains were brought back to the chapel that he had built ten years earlier on Bluff Point for his son, and he was buried in the crypt. He had been in the wine business for sixty-two years, leaving a major impact on the industry and on Yates County during the years he spent here.

15

"WILD BILL" ALBERTSON AND HIS MILLER SPECIAL

The first real sports boom in American history occurred during the Roaring Twenties, and it turned a number of athletes into national icons. There were Babe Ruth and Ty Cobb in baseball, Red Grange and Knute Rockne in football, Bobby Jones and Walter Hagen in golf, Bill Tilden and Helen Wills in tennis and Jack Dempsey and Gene Tunney in boxing. A sports figure who dominated the local scene during the 1920s was Bill Albertson. He was an amateur race car driver who started out on local dirt tracks and, by the mid- to late 1920s, was racing against some of the best known names in the sport—and winning. The high point of his career was when he and a car he owned raced in the Indianapolis 500 in May 1929. The local newspapers of the time, the *Chronicle-Express* and *Penn Yan Democrat*, followed Bill Albertson's every move in racing, and so did the readers they served.

Bill was the son of Danish immigrants who farmed near Geneva. When his father died, his mother moved into Penn Yan with her children. As a young man, he worked as an auto mechanic in different garages in Penn Yan, starting with the one owned by Allen Wagner on East Elm Street. In 1915, he bought his own business on Central Avenue (The building is still there located directly behind Trombley Tire). He got into racing at that same time, driving a Maxwell touring car that he had converted into a race car. He started at the Yates County Fairgrounds and then advanced to dirt tracks throughout central and western New York. In 1920, he modified a Chalmers race car and started to earn a reputation throughout upstate New York. When he bought a Duesenberg racer in 1921 the *Syracuse Post Standard* reported, "If Bill Albertson, a local automobile mechanic, ever can get an automobile that will travel fast enough to suit him, he will be among the peers in the racing game…fans in this section believe Bill will carry away three-fourths of the events on the dirt tracks of New York state this summer." It was at that time that he picked up the nickname "Wild Bill" because it seemed that he would take any chance to win a race. When he finished second at the New York State Fair in Syracuse in 1922 against some of the top racers in the country, his reputation grew throughout the Northeast.

Through the mid-1920s he raced at county fairs and tracks in New York, New Jersey, Pennsylvania and Ohio. Although he was banned from a few tracks because of his reckless driving, he set track records at several others and became a headline attraction wherever he raced. His standing in racing circles progressed so that he could demand a cash guarantee just to compete in a race. By 1927, his reputation had grown to the point that he was scheduled to be a relief driver at the Indianapolis 500 on Memorial Day, but he had to cancel due to the untimely death of his mother-in-law.

In 1928, he bought a 1923 Miller 122 for around $12,000 (the car shown in the photo). Harry Miller of California was a well-known race car builder, and his cars dominated competition during the 1920s and early 1930s. Only thirty-seven of that particular model were made. The car Albertson bought had already run in three Indy 500s and once finished as high as fourth. In Wild Bill's first seven starts with the new car, he set five new track records. The next spring, he felt good enough about the car to enter it in the 1929 Indianapolis 500. Still recovering from injuries from when his car went through the fence at Langhorne racetrack the previous October, Albertson asked Frank Farmer of Pennsylvania to be the primary driver. Albertson would do mechanic duties and be the relief driver. He raced the car in laps 119 to 134, when Farmer took over driving duties again. Car No. 36 developed problems with its supercharger and was forced to drop out of the race on lap 140. It started the race in the twenty-sixth position and went out in fourteenth. Their prize money was $459.

Albertson continued to race his Miller Special for the remainder of 1929, winning one-hundred-mile races at Lehighton and Bloomsburg in Pennsylvania. The next year started out promising enough for Wild Bill, as he scored a win in a one-hundred-mile race in Toledo, Ohio. Through the summer, he raced at Langhorne in Pennsylvania, Woodbridge in New Jersey and on Long Island. The year turned tragic in August, however, when he took his car to the half-mile clay track at the Orange County Fair in Middletown, New York. In a time trial, he was attempting to set a new track record before a crowd of sixteen thousand people. The Middletown newspaper had a dramatic description of what happened:

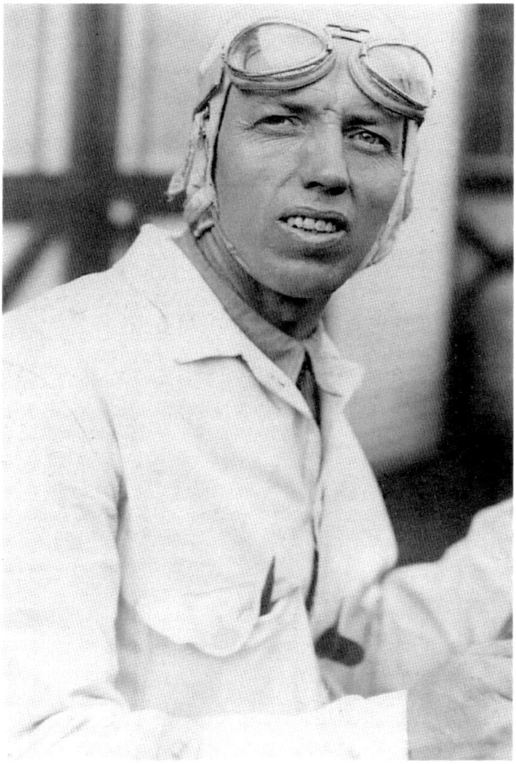

Left: William C. "Wild Bill" Albertson. *Courtesy of YCHC.*

Below: Bill and his Miller Special at the Indy 500. *Courtesy of YCHC.*

> *Finally the wine colored machine was wheeled to the starting line and Albertson tightened his familiar white whipcord helmet. Elmer Gerner, the starter, wished Albertson luck. His wife strolled back behind the judge's stand where she could better watch the trial. In a moment Wild Bill was off for the first preliminary circling of the track. Down the course came the car high on the track for the breathless swerve into the first short turn. Gerner gave him the green starting flag and a dozen watches clicked. It was obvious Albertson's attempt was to be terrifically fast. He pulled the car past the first turn and gave it the gun to the far stretch. At the three-quarters pole stopwatches afterward indicated he was traveling at a 27 second gait or approximately 73 miles per hour in the short straight-away. But as Albertson whisked into the far turn his car suddenly lunged sideways, rolled over once at right angles, and then with tremendous momentum up-ended from the rear and bounced high in the air. Albertson was hurled from the seat, a flying figure with arms and legs spread like a white robed diver plunging from some high springboard. As he neared the ground 40 feet away he seemed to double forward in position practiced by drivers to break falls of less momentum. He hit the track's center on his shoulders and rolled over thrice as though ending swift handsprings. Suddenly he slithered into the guardrail. Under the guiderail lay Albertson, his head crushed. Younger, his mechanic, arrived. He hurried past the blanketed figure and savagely kicked a wheel of the death car, which had stopped upright in center track 75 yards from the first skid marks. The car was little damaged. Preliminary examination disclosed that a right front wheel had apparently frozen and thus had slung the light car into uncontrolled skids.*[9]

At the time of his death, Bill Albertson was forty-two years old. He and his wife lived on Benham Street in Penn Yan, and the community was shocked and saddened by his death. Over fifty friends, neighbors, loyal fans and former customers traveled up to Rochester for his funeral and burial. Elizabeth Albertson sold her husband's car to another driver, and it continued to race into the late 1930s. Then, since Harry Miller only made a few of that particular model, it became a collector's item and passed through a series of collectors in the United States and England. It has been fully restored and was sold at a California estate sale in 2008 for $2,035,000. As of 2009, it was owned by the retired chairman of the Winn-Dixie chain of grocery stores who lives in Florida, and he has taken what was once Wild Bill Albertson's car No. 36 to shows and competitions. It won Best in Show at the prestigious Concours d'Elegance in Amelia Island, Florida, in March 2009.

16

TALES FROM "THE PINES"

French Gold, Ghosts, Hermits, Suburbia and the Klan

From the time Penn Yan became a settled village, the area at the northern end of the East Branch of Keuka Lake was known as "the Pines" for the obvious reason that there was a line of pine trees along the shore. Although the land was mostly privately owned, locals came there in the summer to swim since the water was fairly shallow. It was also a favored area for picnicking and fishing.

The landowner was Uriah Hanford, whose 225 acre farm included quite a stretch of shoreline at the northern end of the East Branch of Keuka Lake, running from where the water plant is today to the entrance of the outlet. His farm stretched from the lake westward over the ridge nearly to the County House Road. The farmhouse was built in the 1820s in the town of Jerusalem just outside Penn Yan. Eventually, it would be on the plank road that went from Penn Yan to Branchport and, after 1897, the Penn Yan, Keuka Park and Branchport electric railway. The house, a private residence, is still there today. One could drive past it a hundred times and never notice it—an old house shrouded by trees and shrubbery on Route 54A at the edge of Penn Yan. Like many homes and farms in Yates County, it has an interesting and diverse history.

Uriah Hanford came to the area from Otsego County in 1823, the year Yates County was legally organized. He married a daughter of Abraham Wagener, another pioneer in the area, and the Hanfords moved onto their farm in 1827. Hanford was primarily a farmer, but he was also involved in the mercantile trade on Main Street in Penn Yan. He was active in local politics,

The "Old Hanford Place" on the edge of Penn Yan. *Author's collection.*

The area at the north end of the east branch of Keuka Lake known as "the Pines," which was then part of the Hanford farm. *Courtesy of YCHC.*

having served as justice of the peace and town supervisor in Jerusalem and county sheriff. Hanford died in May 1875 at the age of seventy-six. His widow and daughter, Mary, continued to live on the farm. Mary eventually married George Eastman, and they lived there into the 1920s.

The Hanford farmland has an extensive history that predates the settlement of the village of Penn Yan. Stafford Cleveland's *History of Yates County* describes significant evidence of an early native burial ground and village along the shoreline there. When it was first developed for farming, large quantities of human bones were discovered along with "brass and copper kettles, rifle barrels, fragments of pottery, tomahawks of both iron and stone, stone pipes, and spear and arrow heads."[10]

Jacob Fredenburg, often said to be the first white man to live in the area that eventually became Penn Yan, lived among those natives for a time in the late 1780s. He met an elderly Frenchman living in their village who did blacksmithing for the natives. As the old story went, the Indians told Fredenburg about buried treasure on the land: "Heap money—much gold." The Frenchman didn't share much information about it with Fredenburg. When he asked the natives where the gold came from, they always pointed to the north. He eventually learned the alleged details: A party of Frenchmen came from Quebec and were working their way to Fort Duquesne (Pittsburgh) and then down the river system to New Orleans. They were carrying with them a large quantity of gold that was said to have been "wrongly acquired." They stopped for a while at the Indian village at the foot of the lake near the entrance to the outlet and did some trading with the natives. For some reason, tension developed between the Frenchmen and the natives, and the leader of the group buried the gold as a precaution. The Senecas did indeed attack the visitors and massacred several of them, including the man who buried the gold. A few of the younger men were spared and adopted into the tribe. One of those continued to live at that location until he was an old man, the one who was still there in the 1780s. Fredenburg passed that story along to his son, and so the story spread. Over the years, many local residents have looked for the treasure, using divining rods and digging. It was said by some of them that the gold was enchanted and moved itself just as someone was about to discover it. Others said that it was guarded by an animal apparition with a long tail. Some said it looked like a lion; others said a calf. No gold was ever found.

At the time of the Civil War, there was a horse racetrack on Hanford's land near the lake, called the Keuka Trotting Park. The county fairgrounds were then located along what is now Keuka Street in Penn Yan and were too small for a decent track. There were meets held a few times a year, but usually, there were match races between local horsemen that brought large crowds to the track.

In the late 1800s into the early 1900s, there were men who lived on the land as "squatters" near the outlet and were known locally as the Hanford Hermits. John Calhoun lived there for over thirty years. He raised sunken logs from the outlet and sold them for lumber. He had several boats that he rented out to fisherman and was an expert fisherman himself. He started out living on a houseboat on the lake, but a storm in the late 1890s blew his boat into the end of the lake at the Pines, wrecking the bottom of the boat but leaving the cabin intact. He made that into a comfortable shack with a view of the lake. "When seen on a summer's night sitting on the miniature porch of his abode, smoking his pipe and gazing across the peaceful waters of Lake Keuka, the picture lingers in one's mind as an ideal of solid comfort," noted the *Yates County Chronicle* of April 1, 1925. Calhoun suffered a stroke and died in 1929 at the age of seventy-six.

Around 1910, another hermit, Howland Snyder, built his shack, facing south looking down the lake, on state-owned land near the entrance to the Keuka Lake outlet. Howland was described in the *Chronicle* as "a local character of more or less prominence." He had a long history of scrapes with the law. They were usually minor offenses: stealing chickens or rags, selling whiskey illegally or using traps to catch pheasants, most of which resulted in local jail time. Local authorities must have loved to see him coming. On the charge of stealing rags to sell, he appeared before a justice of the peace and took charge of his own defense. "He said he had always voted the Republican ticket and inasmuch as several good Republicans have died recently, it would be a shame to send him to jail and deprive the party of his services. After listening to the eloquent plea of the prisoner, the justice adjourned the case," reported the *Yates County Chronicle* of August 11, 1916. At his home in the Pines, he had a small garden and raised chickens and a pig. He also had a notorious cat that would snarl and hiss at boaters as they went in and out of the outlet. Howland worked on nearby farms during the busy times and fished in the lake. "He has books to read and time to read them and while he lives in a very primitive manner, he enjoys life. Many a busy man who has spent his vacation on Lake Keuka and become acquainted with either of the hermits, has afterwards wished, when in the midst of an especially trying time, that he might leave it all and be a hermit on Lake Keuka," said the April 1, 1925 *Yates County Chronicle*. In 1931, nearing the age of eighty and in declining health, Howland was convinced to abandon his shack and go into the county poorhouse, which was the Esperanza Mansion at that time. He died there several months later.

George and Mary Hanford Eastman lived on the farm until 1924. In that year, they sold all but the land immediately around the house and barn, a sizable 170 acres, to a development company from Rochester. The Rochester company turned around and sold it to the recently formed Finger Lakes Land Corporation, whose stockholders were local businessmen and whose president was Paul Ritchey. They planned a housing development on the land and intended to start work in the spring of 1925 to create Penn Yan's "new suburb." As work began on the project, Ritchey ran a contest in local papers to get a name for the new development. There were hundreds of entries, and Ritchey eventually declared two winners: "Indian Gardens" and "Whispering Pines." He then combined the two into "Indian Pines."

That summer some trees were cut down, new trees were planted, the land was divided into lots and streets were laid out. (The street next to Seneca Farms is still called Ritchey Boulevard.) Electricity and water lines were installed, and some sidewalks were put in. By the way, nothing was done to displace the two hermits. Calhoun, having lived there so long, held "squatter's rights," and Snyder lived on state land. According to local papers, the only effect it had on them was "to bring them nearer to the hustle and bustle of the busy world than they like to be."

In late April 1925, the Finger Lakes Land Company began aggressive advertising in all local newspapers. Ninety lots were offered for sale starting on May 9, twenty directly on the lake and seventy elsewhere in the development. The lots not directly on the lake sold for $100 to $500, depending on location. They did not advertise what the lots on the lake sold for, although early in the Depression, that price was lowered to $1,100. The company's land office was the small stucco building diagonally across from Seneca Farms Ice Cream & Restaurant. It is now a private residence.

"'Indian Pines' now laid out with new streets, trees and building lots is fast taking on the appearance of a new residential section. The streets of this new suburb of Penn Yan have been plainly marked with attractive names and many cars of sight-seers were using them for the first time this weekend. This new project promises more prosperity for Penn Yan," reported the *Yates County Chronicle* of May 13, 1925. The advertisement in the paper said: "Picture yourself in a cottage of your own on Keuka's shores. It is the end of a glorious summer day. Silvery moonbeams playing on the water. Myriads of the early evening lights twinkle on the other shore. Wafted to you by the cool and refreshing breezes are the sounds of music, laughter and gayety

INDIAN PINES

A Subdivision of the Hanford Farm and Lake Front

OPENING DAY MAY 9

Overlooking the Lake but Not Touching On It

70 Superb Home Sites

SMALL PAYMENT DOWN BALANCE EASY

TO BE SOLD

10% Discount on all sums paid over the first payment made within thirty days

A FEW LOTS PRICED AS LOW AS $100

All lots have building and set back line restrictions, graded streets, stakes, trees planted. Water pipes are to be laid and sidewalks are to be put down on some streets. Lake Shore Drive (lake road) already has street car line, pavement, water main, telephone line and two electric power lines ready for immediate use.

20 Beautiful Lake Lots ON SALE

Price and Terms of Sale will be given on application

A Shallow Beach is a Safe Beach

Making these lots the most desirable of any on the shores of the Keuka. "Old Pines Trail" leading from Lake Shore Drive (lake road) to the land now being reserved for one year awaiting a decision on a proposed City Park, is to be graded, graveled, sidewalk to be built on the east side of the street, water main to be put in and electric current made available.

$500 in Cash to be Given Home Builders

$300.00 for the First House Built
$150.00 for the Second House Built
$ 50.00 for the Third House Built

Conditions under which prize money will be awarded:

The prize money is considered due and payable to the first three home builders in the order in which they comply with the following: 1st, construct a building in Indian Pines which complies with the building and set back line covenants.

2nd, have the building with roof and chimney complete; all doors and windows in; all porches complete; sided and painted two coats or stucco finish job on; all these before October 15th, 1925.

3rd, purchase or agree to purchase the lot on which it stands in Indian Pines.

Our Representatives will be on the property all day Saturday and every day thereafter to give you information about one of the finest and largest subdivisions ever opened in this vicinity.

For your convenience each lot is numbered and has card tacked on a white stake, giving the lot number and block and the size of the lot, the price and terms. Look them over and when you find one that suits you, tear off the tag and take it to our office at 600 Lake Shore Drive (lake road), which is the tenant house now being remodeled, or give it to a representative on the ground.

SAVE MAY 9th for a visit to Indian Pines. Make your selection early. First choice is always best.

HOW TO GO. Short distance west on Elm street until you can see our signs.

FINGER LAKES LAND CO., Inc., Owners

600 Lake Shore Drive, Penn Yan, N. Y.

Left: Advertisement from the *Yates County Chronicle* in April 1925. *Courtesy of YCHC.*

Opposite: Handbill from the collection of the Yates County History Center. *Courtesy of YCHC*

of a happy and carefree people." Credit was easy—ten dollars down and five dollars or more a month. A 10 percent discount was offered if a lot was bought with cash. Lots sold quickly, and because cash incentives were offered for the first three houses to be completed, construction began immediately.

From the beginning of the project, plans were in place to build a public park at the end of the Pines near the outlet, but the marsh had to be acquired from the heirs of Abraham Wagener's estate, other landowners and the state of New York, which owned land along the outlet. The plan called for a bathing beach at the foot of the lake, picnic grounds and turning the marsh into "a series of miniature islands and lagoons; cleaning up the approaches to it and creating a place of beauty practically unknown in the country, interfering with none of the rights of adjoining owners and making a public eyesore into a place of rare beauty," according to the January 27, 1926 *Yates County Chronicle*.

The Finger Lakes Land Company donated its part of the land in May 1926. A bill was introduced in Albany to have the state give their part of the land to the village of Penn Yan, and Governor Franklin Roosevelt signed that bill in April 1931. But there were complications. The state land was acquired in the 1820s for the construction of the Crooked Lake Canal. The heirs of Abraham Wagener maintained that when the canal went defunct, the land reverted back to their estate. There were leases and flowage rights in the marsh held by the mills down the outlet that had to be addressed. In addition, Penn Yan taxpayers balked at the expense of converting the marsh, which had been a dumping ground for years, into a park lake. It wasn't until the summer of 1942 that all titles were cleared and the village accepted the land for what became Indian Pines Park.

The original Hanford house and barn were sold to Merrill Beach at the same time that the farm was sold to the land company in 1924. Beach was a Ford dealer in Penn Yan. In 1927, he sold the property to an organization called the Lone Pine Club. The club was a front for the Yates County chapter of the Ku Klux Klan. The names of all officers and the members of the board of directors of the club who signed the incorporation papers matched up with known members of the Klan. For two years, the KKK held regular meetings and special rallies at the site. Old-timers remember crosses being burned on the hill behind the house. When the Klan declined locally (and nationally) in 1929, the property was sold back to Merrill Beach, who eventually, in 1937, sold it to Marvin Allison to be used as offices for his roofing business.

The "old Hanford place" is as of 2013 owned by Patty Tinney. I met with Patty in preparation for this chapter and appreciated her input. She told me that the house has been on the state and national Register of Historic Places since 1994. She also said that artifacts were found in a tunnel behind a stairway in the basement, which builds a pretty good case that the house was once a stop on the Underground Railroad (ironic considering the later Klan connection).

17

THE PENN YAN CUBAN GIANTS AND THE 1924 SEASON

In June 1924, the Cuban Giants Baseball Club Inc. of Brooklyn, New York, made a proposal to the Penn Yan Chamber of Commerce in Penn Yan. If the chamber would allow them to use the Yates County Fairgrounds and agree to relocate the ball diamond in front of the grandstand, the Cuban Giants would play at least two home games a week there throughout the summer and adopt the name "Penn Yan Cuban Giants." The fairgrounds in those days were located where the Lake Street Plaza is in Penn Yan today. The team's offer coincided with a wave of "boosterism" throughout business communities in small towns across America during the 1920s, including Penn Yan. The chamber of commerce and the county agricultural society (which oversaw the fairgrounds) saw the opportunity to bring business into the village and promote the name of Penn Yan, so the deal was made. The first game was played a week later.

The Cuban Giants were a semiprofessional team of mainly minor-league talent. The New York City area had three major-league teams playing in the Eastern Colored League at the time: the New York Cuban Stars, the New York Lincoln Giants and the Brooklyn Royal Giants. Add to that the Brooklyn Dodgers, New York Giants and New York Yankees of the major leagues, and the baseball market downstate was quite saturated. The Cuban Giants figured that there was more money to be made upstate, where there was much less competition. Plus, they were somewhat familiar with Penn Yan, having come through there on barnstorming tours over the years, and they believed it to be a good baseball town.

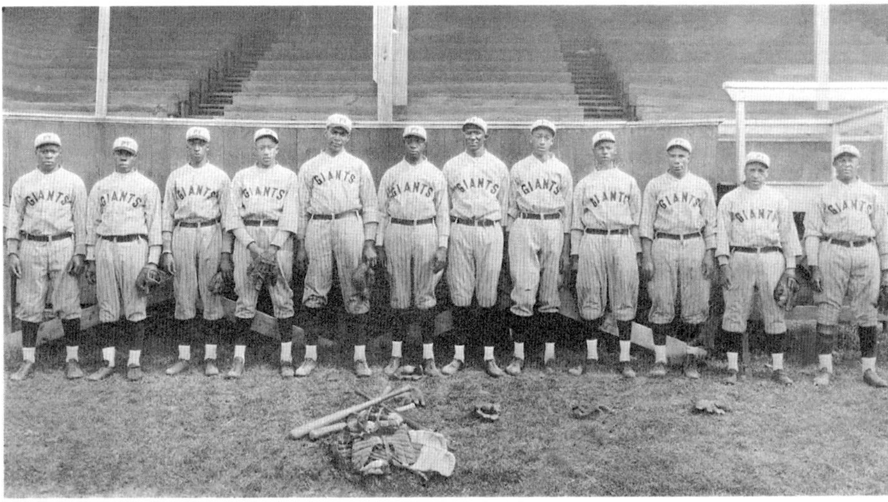

The Penn Yan Cuban Giants at the Yates County Fairgrounds, 1925. *Courtesy of YCHC.*

The Cuban Giants guaranteed visiting teams fifty to one hundred dollars to come to Penn Yan for a game. What was left from the gate revenues was used to cover team expenses and pay the players and coaches of the home team. Therefore, the success of the whole operation depended on getting people out to the ballpark. Tickets were fifty cents, and the business community, including the local newspapers, worked to encourage people to go out and see our "national sport." As the *Penn Yan Democrat* put it: "It is now up to the people of Penn Yan to show whether they want baseball or not, and the attendance at the games will be your answer." The *Yates County Chronicle* wrote, "The Cuban Giants are a good bunch of players and an orderly bunch of men and are worthy of your patronage. They cannot play baseball unless they have your support at the games."

There were no Cubans on the Cuban Giants. Black teams used that name going back into the 1880s because it was believed that white baseball fans would watch Latin American players before they would watch black ones. The team was managed by John B. Johnson and included players like "Beano" Thomas, "Chick" Wells, Rufus Johnson, William "Baldy" Woods and Richard "George" Washington. The players were from everywhere but here—southern states and the cities of the East Coast. They wanted to play ball and make a little money in the process. During the 1924 season, they played teams from all over western New York and northern Pennsylvania; other semipro teams, industrial teams, town teams, all-star teams—whoever would put up the money.

They played eighty-nine games in 1924, winning sixty-two of them. Their first game was played at the Yates County Fairgrounds in late June against the "Imperials" of Painted Post, an Ingersoll-Rand Corporation team. The *Yates County Chronicle* described it: "The first game of baseball played by the Cuban Giants was a success from the standpoint of amusement, although not a financial success. Every person who saw the game is enthusiastic and the antics of the Cuban Giants were producers of laughs equal to a minstrel show." The game was a laugh also. The Cuban Giants won 15–5. From then on, they played at home each Thursday at 5:00 p.m. and Saturday at 3:30 p.m. They played on the road on all other days except Sundays. From the start, they suffered from low attendance. At that first game, they took in $84 at the gate. From that, they had to pay the visiting team their $50 guarantee, and after paying for equipment and advertising, very little was left for the players. After a home game against the Lehigh Valley Shopmen from Sayre, Pennsylvania, in July, the *Chronicle* reported, "Saturday's crowd was the largest which has attended any of the ball games so far. The receipts, however, were but $162 and the Giants had to pay the visitors $100. After paying for the bats and balls out of the remaining $62, it was mighty lean bacon that the Penn Yan men had to chew on." Low turnout and low gate receipts plagued the team throughout the season.

The season ended with a bang in September. During the county fair, the Cuban Giants attracted large crowds as they played Seneca Falls and Geneva teams. The ball games, the horse races and other attractions gave the 1924 Yates County Fair a record-breaking attendance. The real highlight at the end of the season, however, was playing the Toronto Maple Leafs of the International League on September 16. Toronto had a four-day gap in its schedule, and the man who booked teams for the Cuban Giants was able to bring the Maple Leafs to Penn Yan to play an exhibition game for a guarantee of $250. Before a large crowd, the home team was defeated 14–8, but the paper reported that they were "competitive" throughout the game. They played their last game that season on September 20 against Lodi and then played their way south to their spring training base in Orangeburg, South Carolina, where they broke up until the following spring. Seven of the players actually returned to Penn Yan to get jobs and spend the winter. The season ended, however, on a controversial note. The man who booked the Toronto game was arrested for grand larceny as some of the Giant players charged him with withholding some of the gate receipts. In spite of that, it was a pretty good season for the team, but the papers ominously reported: "Whether or not they return to Penn Yan next season is not yet decided."

The decision was made over the winter; the Cuban Giants relocated to Maryland for the 1925 season, but the seven players who stayed in Penn Yan that winter decided to form a new team so they could play there and stay in Penn Yan. They did fundraising in the area over the winter, putting on dances and concerts (they proved to have musical talent in addition to baseball), and attracted financial backing from Penn Yan businessmen. They hired a new manager who recruited additional players, and they played that season as the Penn Yan Colored Giants. The uniforms shown in the photo on page 120 were gray with green pinstripes, and the Giants' bench sweaters were cadet blue. Once again, they found out that home games in Penn Yan were not profitable enough to meet expenses, and they ended the season by barnstorming throughout the northeast. At the end of the season, the members of the team went their separate ways, with the exception of Rufus Johnson, who stayed in Penn Yan and raised his family. Johnson did shoe shines in several barbershops and hotels around the village and played on a few different town and company baseball teams until age caught up with him. He earned quite a reputation as "the Charleston King" at dances. Rufus Johnson died in 1962 at the age of sixty-six and is buried in Lakeview Cemetery in Penn Yan.

18
YATES COUNTY AND THE KLAN

I had this topic marinating in my mind for several years. In doing family history research, I ran across the fact that my grandparents who lived in Penn Yan were active in the Ku Klux Klan in the 1920s. Being troubled by that fact, I was driven to do research on the Klan throughout upstate New York and specifically in Yates County. I have gone through every issue of the three major local newspapers—the *Yates County Chronicle*, which became the *Chronicle-Express* in 1926; the *Penn Yan Democrat*; and the *Dundee Observer*—from 1923 to 1930. I have interviewed a surviving Klan member and have information from other interviews with people who remember the era. I have gone through local Klan minutes from 1925 through 1927. What I have found will surprise people not familiar with social attitudes of the 1920s and may make others understand, as I have come to, why their family members might have been involved with the KKK in the 1920s.

To start with, the 1920s were peak years for national Klan membership and influence. It was estimated that there were around 6 million members in the mid-1920s. Although the national leadership was generally southern, the Klan at that time became largely a northern and midwestern organization. There were a number of reasons for that. By the time of World War I, cities in the North were filled with recently arrived immigrants from southern and Eastern Europe, many of whom were Catholic or Jewish. The war accelerated the Great Migration of rural southern African Americans into the industrial cities of the North. Added to this was the general disillusionment that Americans had with foreigners as a result of the involvement in the war

Local Klan Handbook in the YCHC collection. *Courtesy of YCHC.*

and its aftermath, including the Bolshevik Revolution in Russia in 1917. The result was a major emphasis on being "100 percent American," which meant at that time white, Anglo-Saxon and Protestant. The ten years following the end of World War I was a very intolerant period in this country.

In upstate New York, the catalyst for the rise of the Klan was Governor Al Smith, who served between 1923 and 1928. Al Smith was everything that rural and small-town upstate New York was not. He was a Democrat, a political progressive, a Roman Catholic, a "wet" who opposed Prohibition and very urban, speaking with a thick New York City accent. He was backed by what was left of Tammany Hall, the New York City political "machine" that most New Yorkers associated with corruption. Al Smith was elected governor four times, but his popularity was almost entirely downstate. In Yates County when he ran for reelection in 1926, Al Smith got 1,660 votes while his Republican opponent got 4,830. When he ran for the presidency in 1928 against Herbert Hoover, his vote in Yates was 1,940 to Hoover's 7,376.

The first reports of Klan activity in Yates County came early in 1924. The *Penn Yan Democrat* reported in February that a cross was burned near Potter, and Klan literature was left at the site. A month later, the same paper wrote:

> *The western part of the county seems to be a hotbed for Ku Klux Klan activities. Potter and Middlesex are especially rampant with burning crosses and open meetings. It is rumored that two prominent citizens of Potter journeyed to New York City recently to be initiated into the higher degrees of Klan work with expectations of becoming organizers throughout this section. Upon their return they said that the sights which were revealed to them in the great metropolis were varied and almost unbelievable.*

The organizers must have done their jobs, as the *Democrat* reported on August 1: "The Ku Klux Klan formed several societies in this county during the past few weeks. One is located in Penn Yan." A week later, the *Yates County Chronicle* included this: "The Ku Klux Klan has held four open meetings in this vicinity during the past two weeks—at Potter July 20th, Bellona July 22nd, Yatesville July 24th, and one near Hall on July 29th. It is estimated that from one thousand to fifteen hundred attended each meeting." In September the *Chronicle* added, "It is well known that some 300 cars took approximately 1200 people to a meeting last Friday night addressed by a Dr. Minor of Dallas Texas, who is said to be one of the national organizers and lecturers of the Klan. This meeting was held on a farm in the town of Jerusalem." In Penn Yan that October, there was a meeting at the Masonic Hall. Over 800 people came to listen to a Klan lecturer from Atlanta, Georgia.

A number of years ago, I interviewed an elderly woman who was in the Penn Yan KKK along with her husband. When I asked her why she joined, she mentioned Al Smith as the primary reason, as well as the fact that her minister was a member. When I asked her what she remembered about the meetings she mentioned singing hymns and patriotic songs, saluting the American flag and saying prayers. She remembered picnics, potluck suppers, field days, parades and playing cards after the meetings. She emphasized the fraternal and social aspects of the organization. Klan members took care of sick members who needed help. They took up collections for members down on their luck. They sent flowers to members for births, anniversaries, weddings and funerals. I finally asked her if they burned crosses, and she said, "Oh, yes!"

The KKK has been called "the Invisible Empire," but in Yates County, it was semitransparent. An old-timer was interviewed a while back who told of hiding in the bushes outside of Klan meetings as a young boy to get a look at who attended.[11] In September 1924, the *Penn Yan Democrat* reported, "There was a big meeting of KKKs out in the country Friday night. Several young men who went out to attend the meeting were not permitted to enter. They started back to Penn Yan and on their way they stopped to see who was passing. They recognized quite a few of our leading citizens as they passed by." Klan membership included workers and farmers but also a few deputy sheriffs, school administrators, village officials, businessmen and (according to the woman I interviewed) Protestant ministers.

As far as my grandfather goes, as a member of one of the volunteer fire departments in Penn Yan as well as Company O, the Yates County home guard unit in World War I, I believe he saw himself as protecting the quality of life in the community. Many of the men who served in the fire department and the home guard unit with him were also in the Klan. Add to that the nativism and bigotry that were common to his generation and those times, and I have come to better understand why my grandparents were involved. The Klansmen saw themselves as defenders of Americanism, Protestantism, white supremacy, Prohibition and traditional "American values."

In what types of activities were Klan members involved? I will say up front that I found no information in the newspapers that linked the local Klan to any crime being committed in the area. It did, however, use blatant fear and intimidation. In addition to members' dressing in full regalia for Klan activities, crosses were burned throughout the county. I found specific reports of crosses being burned at the Yates County Fairgrounds in Penn Yan, near Rushville and Dundee, at the end of Bluff Point, on the hill above the Esperanza and on farms in Benton, Starkey, Potter, Jerusalem and Milo. A favorite spot was on a hill between Penn Yan and Dresden known locally at that time as "Nigger Hill" and referred to as such by the local newspapers. Members paraded in full regalia in Penn Yan, Canandaigua, Hornell, Horseheads, Geneva and Binghamton. In October 1924, the *Yates County Chronicle* reported "Some 50 cars bearing electrically lighted crosses and carrying klansmen and klan sympathizers paraded through the main streets of Penn Yan last Saturday night. Where the cars came from and where they went is apparently a mystery, although many reports and rumors were about. It was also said that many more cars paraded the streets of

Dundee." They were coming from a meeting on a farm out on Pre-emption Road. It was reported that a couple of young men from Penn Yan were arrested for putting tacks on the road leading to the meeting, which resulted in several flat tires. That same night the *Corning Leader* reported:

> *It is alleged that on Saturday evening Trooper Porter stopped twenty-five cars at Painted Post containing 100 members of the Corning Ku Klux Klan en route to a meeting near Dundee and took KKK banners, crosses, emblems, and American flags from the cars. It is alleged that the trooper did not give any reason for his act other than saying "you ought to be ashamed of yourself." After nearly twenty minutes, the Klansmen were allowed to continue on their way.*

In June 1925, the Penn Yan Klan hosted a "Klonverse" at the Yates County Fairgrounds. It was a two-day meeting of KKK organizations from fourteen counties in central and western New York. The *Penn Yan Democrat* reported that it was the first public demonstration by the Klan in Penn Yan, and "more than ordinary interest was aroused." An estimated eight to ten thousand people attended the event. There were speeches by leaders from the national organization, several cross burnings and food provided by the women's auxiliary. Private ceremonies were held that included the induction of over one hundred new members into the Klan. A highlight was a parade down Main Street to the fairgrounds with over five hundred Klansmen in full regalia accompanied by two bands, four hooded "knights" on horseback and a car with state Klan leaders. The *Democrat* wrote that "more people were on the streets to witness this parade than have gathered here in years. The parade was undisturbed and quiet except for occasional applause from onlookers." On the first day of the Klonverse, a cross was burned on the lawn of a black man who lived on Jackson Street in the village. It was put out by the fire department, and the local Klan disclaimed all responsibility. Later, according to Klan minutes, one of its members was reprimanded in a meeting and fined ten dollars for unauthorized cross burning. It had its standards.

The Klan held regular meetings at a variety of places in and around Penn Yan. It had field days, special ceremonies and cross burnings out on neighboring farms. In town, it met at the Masonic Lodge, the Grange Hall, the Moose Club, the Methodist Church and the Baptist Church. A February 1925 issue of the Penn Yan Democrat described a show of appreciation for one of the Klan's meeting places:

The "Klonverse" at the Yates County Fairgrounds, 1925. *Courtesy of YCHC.*

Mounted Klansmen at the Yates County Fairgrounds. *Courtesy of YCHC.*

> *At the Sunday evening service in the Methodist Church twelve uniformed members of the Yates County Ku Klux Klan entered the church and marched down the main aisle and presented Rev. Houghton, the pastor, with a packet containing $50 to be used for the Methodist home for children in Williamsville. The audience, which packed the large auditorium, was just closing the service by the singing of America as the men came in. At the request of Rev. Houghton they sang the first verse of America and knelt at the altar and offered a short prayer. After a few words from the leader in tendering the gift, the men left the church quietly and disappeared.*

Starting in 1927 they met at the Lone Pine Club, which was the house on the old Hanford farm near Indian Pines just outside Penn Yan.

The Penn Yan KKK had a women's auxiliary. It called itself the Ku Ka Klub and met at the same time as the men, but in a separate room. There were 193 names on their membership list. Reading though their minutes, they could have been a sewing circle, a literary club or a prayer group. They took care of the social niceties for the whole organization. They sent cards and flowers to members. They prepared food for special dinners and events. They took care of buying the robes (a Klan robe in the mid-1920s cost $3.50). They opened their meetings with hymns. Sometimes it was a traditional one: "Old Rugged Cross" or "Blessed Be the Tie That Binds." Sometimes it was Klan adapted: "Let the Fiery Cross Keep Burning" or "Stand Up Ye Klansmen." They saluted the flag and sang "The Star Spangled Banner." They had craft lessons and listened to speakers from the state and national level. Their members offered songs and music at meetings and patriotic readings. They put together a list of "approved" Protestant-owned businesses in town, and when the fire department was called to the fairgrounds during the Klonverse because of burning crosses, the secretary mentioned in the minutes that "the truck came to the grounds but did not enter. The truck was loaded with Catholic wops." For all the social niceties, one is constantly reminded that it was a hate group.

The local Klan declined in the late 1920s along with the national organization. There were a number of factors responsible for that. In 1925, at the peak of Klan influence, a national leader (Grand Dragon D.C. Stephenson) was found guilty of a horrific murder of a young woman in Indiana and that disillusioned many members who saw themselves as law-abiding citizens defending American values. The southern Klan, which practiced much more excessive and violent tactics, added to that disillusionment. Some historians believe that the economic prosperity of the late 1920s influenced people to move on to other interests. The last mention of Klan activity in a local newspaper was in January 1928, when they held an oyster supper at the Lone Pine Club just outside Penn Yan. That year was also the year that Al Smith stepped down as the governor of New York to run for the presidency, a race he was destined to lose to Hoover in a landslide.

In closing, I was impressed with this quotation from a webpage of Assumption College's E Pluribus Unum project. It summed up the Ku Klux Klan of the 1920s as well as anything:

> *In the end, the Klan was important not for what it did but for what it signified. It accomplished little but it expressed the otherwise inarticulate*

rage and resentment of millions. At bottom, its members' quarrel was with modernity. In particular, they objected to the rise of Catholics and Jews to positions of power and prominence; they feared that science would undermine the moral authority of the Bible; they worried that a "New Woman" would refuse to submit to patriarchal authority; they worried that a "New Negro" would reject white supremacy. In matters trivial and profound they found themselves threatened with being passed by. The Klan captured perfectly their simultaneous sense of being entitled and endangered.[12]

19
FDR AND YATES COUNTY

In any survey I have ever seen in which historians or political scientists rank the greatest presidents in American history, Franklin D. Roosevelt is ranked among the top three, along with Washington and Lincoln. He guided us through the two biggest crises of the twentieth century—the Great Depression and the Second World War—and we came through both of them in pretty good shape. When FDR died in 1945, a generation of Americans mourned. For many young people, he was the only president they had ever known, having served for twelve years. Yet whatever appeal he may have had around the country and around the world, it didn't apply to Yates County. Six times his name was on the ballot here. He won all of those races overwhelmingly, but he never carried Yates County. Twice he ran for governor, in 1928 and again in 1930. In 1930, he campaigned twice in Yates County and came in a poor third in the county behind the Republican and a third-party candidate. The headline in the *Chronicle-Express* for that election read, "Governor Franklin Roosevelt Carries New York State with Largest Majority Ever Recorded." That same pattern followed for each of Roosevelt's four presidential elections, all huge victories nationwide and statewide but not even close in Yates County. Let's look back at the early days of the Great Depression and the impact of New Deal policies on the county.

The stock market crash of October 1929 apparently had minimal impact on the people of Yates County, since there was very little discussion of it in the local papers. The first mention of hard times came one year later. The October 3, 1930 edition of the *Chronicle-Express* reported:

Governor Franklin D. Roosevelt in front of the Benham Hotel on Main Street in Penn Yan in July 1930. *Courtesy of YCHC.*

> *Numbers of men are walking the highways of the county in quest of work. Especially in the grape section is this true, with 30 applicants for each job that may be vacant. The low prices offered for grapes makes the harvesting of that crop a serious proposition to the growers and the grapes are being picked with as little outlay as possible. Many types of men are seen. Some are the regulation "transients" while the majority of them are clean, respectable appearing men with small bundles under their arms, all seeking jobs. A number of older men, ranging in age from 55 to 70 are seen this year. Penn Yan Police Chief Fitzwater was obliged to request the numbers which congregate in the village to move on, as their numbers were increasing each day. The unemployment problem continues to be as serious as it has been during the past months.*

Conditions worsened through 1931 and 1932. It was estimated that by the end of 1932, one thousand men were out of work in Yates County. "Going Out of Business" sales were prevalent on Main Street. Major area employers like Whitfield & Sons (bus manufacturers) and the Walker Bin Company declared bankruptcy and closed their doors. The *Chronicle-Express* offered free advertising for unemployed men looking for work and announced that they would take certain farm crops in barter exchange for subscriptions to their paper. (They offered an exchange rate 40 percent higher than the market.) Ads in the paper encouraged people to spend money, pay their bills and "Keep Money Moving." The American Legion put on a communitywide drive to find jobs for the unemployed, declaring it a "war on depression." Penn Yan village trustees and Penn Yan teachers independently agreed to give back 10 percent of their salaries in order to prevent tax increases.

At the lowest point of this downward economic spiral came the presidential election of 1932. Herbert Hoover ran for a second term. His words to businessmen in 1932 that "prosperity is just around the corner" rang hollow across the country as shanty towns of the unemployed became known as "Hoovervilles" and newspapers used to protect the homeless from the cold were called "Hoover blankets." In the worst domestic crisis since the Civil War—with World War I veterans (Bonus Marchers) camped out on the Capitol Mall in Washington hinting at revolution and intellectuals singing the praises of fascism or communism—the Democratic nominee for president, Franklin D. Roosevelt, promised Americans a "New Deal." So how did Yates County vote in the presidential election of 1932? Hoover carried the county 6,043 to 2,398 for Roosevelt. The electoral vote across the country was 472 for FDR and 59 for Hoover; 57 percent for FDR to 40 percent for Hoover in the popular vote.

In those days presidents weren't inaugurated until March 4. That day, in his first official action, FDR declared a "Bank Holiday" and ordered all banks closed for a week while Congress acted to stem the banking crisis. In Penn Yan, Citizens Bank and Baldwins Bank had a front-page ad in the *Chronicle* reassuring people that they had enough cash on hand to handle all transactions when they were allowed to reopen. "We shall endeavor to continue to serve your requirements with faith in our financial strength and in the intelligence of our depositors," the ad said. Although both banks were ready to open on the tenth, they didn't receive the go ahead until March 15. There had been no run on the banks in Penn Yan.

Over the next three months (the "100 Days"), the president and Congress passed fifteen major pieces of legislation, a standard against which all presidents since then have been measured. In those first one hundred days, the heart of the New Deal was put in place, and a number of government agencies—known around the country as "alphabet soup"—were created, including the Agricultural Adjustment Act (AAA), the National Recovery Administration (NRA), the Works Progress Administration (WPA), the Public Works Administration (PWA), the Federal Deposit Insurance Corporation (FDIC), the Federal Emergency Relief Administration (FERA) and the Civilian Conservation Corps (CCC). They all had an impact on Yates County.

The NRA's purpose was to end what FDR called "destructive competition" among businesses that drove prices down, profits down and, eventually, led to bankruptcy. Businesses were encouraged to sign onto a "code of fair practices," which mainly regulated prices, hours of operation and wages. Businesses that did so were allowed to display the Blue Eagle, the NRA symbol. They were given a Blue Eagle flag and posters, and they were allowed to display them on their advertising and stationary. FDR then encouraged the public to shop only where they saw the Blue Eagle. The *Chronicle-Express* published long lists of local businesses that cooperated with the NRA under the heading "We Do Our Part." There was an NRA Compliance Board in Penn Yan that fielded and investigated complaints of violations. It had the power to take a blue eagle away from a business, the loss of which was then published in local papers. Until it was declared unconstitutional in 1935, the program did much to stabilize the business community.

The WPA gave a lot of Yates County men work on useful projects around the county. WPA funds hired Yates County men to construct East Bluff Drive from Keuka Park to the end of Bluff Point, tear up the old electric railway tracks on Elm Street in Penn Yan and grade the lakeside banks at

Red Jacket Park, and 200 men were hired to work on state lands in the town of Italy (the High Tor Wildlife Management Area). They did sidewalk work, repaved streets and installed water mains and sewers. A local WPA official reported to the Penn Yan Rotary Club that between November 1935 and April 1936, 166 men were taken from relief rolls and hired to work on twelve projects with a total of $44,000 in grants.

The AAA helped farmers of the county, although meetings had to be held in the county courthouse to explain to farmers how being paid by the government to grow less would cause their income to rise to a level at which they could once again make a living. Farm prices were on their way back up until the AAA was declared unconstitutional in 1936. Despite its unconstitutional ruling, the AAA, in addition to funds from the Rural Electrification Administration that brought power lines to the towns of Starkey, Milo and Torrey for the first time, led to modernization of the farms in the area.

Local newspapers continually ran lists of names of young men who had signed up for the CCC. These men were paid one dollar a day to work on projects throughout the Finger Lakes Region.

FDR and the Democrat-controlled Congress pushed for the end of Prohibition, and when sale of liquor became legal again on December 5, 1933, there was much activity at local wine cellars as wineries hired back men for the work. Increased demand meant that grape prices edged up, which also helped area farmers.

The Federal Housing Administration (FHA) made low-interest mortgages available to people to buy homes. An ad in the *Chronicle-Express* ran, "President Roosevelt says Repair, Rebuild, Repaint and Modernize your home through the Federal Housing Administration." The ad included a list of Penn Yan businesses, carpenters, decorators, masons, plumbers and electricians who agreed to do work for prices set by the FHA. There was a Penn Yan Better Housing Survey Committee that went house to house giving out information for the program. People could borrow money at "unusually low rates" for the work.

By the end of 1936 (and the end of FDR's first term in office), the local economy was beginning to recover from the depths of the Depression. Main Street businesses in Penn Yan were doing much better. Baldwin's Bank enlarged, remodeled and had a grand reopening that fall. The Elmwood Theater was bought by the Schine theater empire and was given a major upgrade. Walkerbilt showed an increase in orders and offered more stable employment to their employees. A major new power plant was planned for

FDR and his New Deal Programs. *Public domain.*

the shores of Seneca Lake near Dresden. Farm prices were rising. With all that, how did FDR do in the 1936 presidential election against Republican Alf Landon of Kansas? FDR: 2,074; Landon: 6,208. FDR got 189 votes fewer than he did four years earlier, and Landon got 850 votes more than Hoover did in 1932.

How does one explain the disconnect between FDR's general popularity and his lack of support in Yates County? The obvious answer is that Yates County has been a conservative Republican stronghold ever since the Republican Party formed in 1854. Even before FDR, the Democratic Party was seen as representing urban interests, catering to the immigrant vote—which included Jews and Catholics—and being opposed to Prohibition, all of which ran contrary to the majority of voters' preferences in rural Yates County. Upstate New York Democrats had the additional handicap of being associated with Tammany Hall in New York City, the political machine that ran the city for decades and was widely associated with political corruption.

I think, however, that part of the answer can be explained by using my grandfather as an example. He was the breadwinner for his family of nine children during the worst years of the Depression. He worked for the Walker Bin Company in Penn Yan, and in the years before it declared bankruptcy, he was laid off for long periods of time when there were no contracts for work. When the company reorganized as Walkerbilt in 1934, there were still long periods with no work, and there was no unemployment insurance in those days. He was a furniture refinisher and did beautiful work. When unemployed, he rode his pickup truck around the county looking for old pieces of furniture that he could buy for a few bucks. He'd take them home, refinish them and sell them for a nice profit. He hunted to feed his family. All his children remembered the squirrel potpie that their mother made. He had a huge garden in his backyard, and my grandmother stocked their basement with canned and preserved vegetables and fruit. A neighbor lady held the mortgage on his house, and one of his daughters clearly remembered her father going to the lady and, with tears in his eyes, explaining that he could only pay the interest on the mortgage and could not afford to pay on the principle. He absolutely refused to take public assistance. In his mind, to do so would have indicated his failure as a man. I think that sense of pride, self reliance and rugged individualism was typical of many Yates County voters and helps to explain why FDR and the Democrats stood so poorly among the voters here.

By the way, when FDR ran for a third term in 1940 against Wendell Wilkie of Indiana, the results in the county were Wilkie with 7,085 and FDR with 1,908. And in 1944, when he ran against Tom Dewey, a very popular Republican New York governor, the results were Dewey with 6,317 and FDR with 1,893. In six elections, Roosevelt never came close to carrying Yates County.

PART IV

1940 TO 1960

20

THE CRASH OF MILLIGAN'S RATS

The Saturday afternoon of October 2, 1943, was unusually cold and foggy on Italy Hill. A local farmer later said that the fog "was so thick you couldn't see a cow 10 feet away." The quiet of that Saturday afternoon was suddenly shattered around 2:30 p.m. Residents in Italy Valley saw a silver army bomber flying low below the clouds and then heard a loud crash. The crash occurred on Italy Hill, the highest point in Yates County with an elevation of 2,130 feet, not far from the Jerusalem town line. The airplane had burrowed into a pasture on a farm that had been abandoned for decades, known locally as "the old Isaac Wilcox farm." Roads in the area had been long abandoned and the only way to get to the area was to walk two miles through overgrown brush and waist-high grass. The first people on the scene saw a one-thousand-foot swath of debris from the point of impact. It was immediately obvious that there were no survivors. The broken bodies of all on board the plane were thrown clear of the wreckage before it burned. According to the *Chronicle-Express* of October 7:

> *About half way along the path plowed in the peaceful pasture, the one wing broke loose and the fully inflated life raft was thrown clear with fire extinguisher and other equipment intact, bright new manila rope trailing over the side, it rested at ease on the rolling sea of grass, its real mission forever unaccomplished. One motor bounced and rolled some 400 feet from the track made by the sliding bomber; the other was over the hill and out of sight in the opposite direction. Three partially opened chute packs lay in white drifts, their soft silk folds billowing gently in the cold breeze that swept along the desolate hill.*

The plane was a twin-engined Mitchell B-25A army air corps bomber. As was the custom of the time, it had been named by one of its earlier pilots. The name was Milligan's Rats. It had taken off that morning from Chatham Field near Savannah, Georgia, on a training run with a crew of five. The pilot was twenty-six-year-old Lieutenant Willard Wilder from Rochester, who must have had some say in the flight plan. The plane landed in Rochester to refuel and pick up a passenger, a tech sergeant from Buffalo who had been home on leave to see his mother and was hopping a ride back to Georgia. They took off from Rochester to begin the return flight to Chatham Field. Lieutenant Wilder's parents had a summer home in the Bristol Hills near Canandaigua Lake, and the young pilot brought his plane in low to drop a weighted note at his parent's place. The note, which they received, read, "See you again someday soon. Take good care of yourselves. Goodbye for a while. Love, Bill." He then dipped his wings in salute and headed south. Milligan's Rats never regained the altitude it needed. It was estimated that with another ten feet, the plane would have cleared Italy Hill.

As word of the crash spread, would-be rescuers and curiosity seekers made their way through the brush for two miles to see the wreckage. There were also souvenir hunters. Service revolvers of the crew members were missing (later turned in to police) as were amounts of ammunition and equipment from the plane. The first officials on the scene were a state trooper from the Penn Yan substation and two other troopers from the Oneida barracks who happened to be visiting in the office when the call came in. They were on the scene just before 5:00 p.m. and were soon joined by Yates County sheriff's deputies. They brought the county coroner in to identify the bodies and clear them to be removed from the scene. Brush and trees were cleared to allow ambulances to the crash site, and the bodies were taken to Thayer Funeral Home in Penn Yan. The army had been notified, and it sent two National Guardsmen to guard the scene of the wreckage for inspectors to look over. They arrived around midnight Saturday night.

The next day, larger crowds came to the crash scene as word spread farther and created quite a challenge to the men guarding the wreckage. According to the *Chronicle-Express*:

> *They had their hands full keeping the curious from walking along the tracks plowed by the plane and further confusing evidence which Army officials wished kept intact pending their investigation. No closer than 500 feet were the orders, but the perverse public insisted upon trying to find ways to circumvent this rule. One young man came up from the valley on horseback and was riding happily*

Illustration of the B-25A bomber over Italy Hill done by Mark Stash, editor of *Life in the Finger Lakes* magazine. *Courtesy of* Life in the Finger Lakes.

> *about the wingtip on the brow of the hill when one of the soldiers first discovered him. "Now where in hell did he come from?" questioned the disgruntled soldier, explaining that he and his buddy had volunteered for this job of guard duty and after 16 hours on the job with no relief, in the biting autumn wind on a bleak hilltop and no hot food, they were getting rather fed up.*

On Sunday night, large army crash trucks arrived from Syracuse and, after cutting some timber, made it to the scene. The investigation was wrapped up on Monday, and the wreckage was removed to Syracuse. The army smoothed the area over and planted some pine trees before leaving. The six bodies were given an honor guard by the local American Legion post until Monday evening. Lieutenant Wilder's parents came to Penn Yan to claim their son's remains, and the other five crew members were taken to the army airfield in Syracuse to be flown to their respective homes.

In 1992, Clarence Sebring and Buster Brewer of Dundee, accompanied by then editor of the Dundee *Observer*, Mary Geo Tomion, ventured back to the scene of the crash of Milligan's Rats. They had gone through quite a lot to identify the exact spot of the crash. The pasture of 1943 had become heavily wooded over the years. Using metal detectors, they were able to unearth several small parts from the bomber. The other result of their expedition was a nice story in the December 9, 1992 issue of the *Observer*.

21

DUANE EDDY'S YATES COUNTY YEARS

I have always loved to listen to music. I've gone through the vinyl stage, cassettes and CDs (somehow I missed 8-tracks), and I sit here today with over five thousand songs in my iTunes library on my iPhone. I often think back to those first vinyl albums I bought in my teen years. I still have them: the Everly Brothers, Buddy Holly, Johnny Cash and the rest. Among them is an album by Duane Eddy, *Have Twangy Guitar, Will Travel*, that I bought in 1958. I generally preferred vocals over instrumentals, but there was something about Duane Eddy's twangy guitar that drilled straight into my adolescent soul with songs such as "Rebel Rouser," "Detour," "Cannonball" and the others. I followed him though the early 1960s when he did great covers of the themes from *Peter Gunn* and *Have Gun—Will Travel*. Then, for me at least, he got lost amid the folk music craze of the mid-'60s, the Beatles and the Rolling Stones.

Fast-forward fifty years. I'm sitting at a table at the Yates County Genealogical & Historical Society annual meeting and dinner in 2011, and a few folks are reminiscing about growing up in the Guyanoga Valley. The name Duane Eddy came up; my ears perked up. One fellow remembered hearing him sing at the Grange Hall in Guyanoga when he was a kid. Back when I was a Duane Eddy fan, I was a teenager in New Jersey, just outside New York City. I was really surprised to hear that he grew up (in part) outside Branchport and went to school in Penn Yan. I looked him up, got a mailing address and an e-mail address and tried to make contact. I first heard from his wife, who told me Duane was performing in Las Vegas and would get back to me when

Teacher Viola Trimmingham's class at Jerusalem School No. 14. Duane Eddy is second from the right on the first row. *Courtesy of YCHC.*

he returned. He's still touring and had a busy summer schedule. He finally did get back to me with the photos and interview that follow:

Q: In what years did you live in Yates County?
A: I lived there from 1949 to 1951. We moved there from Bath, New York. I was born in Corning, New York.

Q: What did your family do here? Someone said that your father had a store in Guyanoga? Did you live in the same building as the store?
A: Yes, we lived behind the store. The store was small but contained a good selection of canned goods, cereals and breads, along with fresh vegetables, meats and ice cream. There were also two gasoline pumps and a kerosene pump in front of the store.

Q: Where did you go to school while here?
A: When I first moved there I was in the sixth grade and went for one semester to a small three-room schoolhouse in Branchport, New York. There were

two grades in each room, and the teachers did an amazing job of handling those two classes at once. I also remember them taking us across the road into the woods for bird-watching classes. There was one quite powerful set of binoculars, and we all took turns looking at different species of birds through the glasses and were able to see them at close range. Seeing the colors and learning the names of the different birds was extremely interesting and fun at the time.

Q: It is well remembered here that you designed the logo for the Penn Yan Mustangs. What do you remember about that?
A: I was in the seventh or eighth grade, and one day, a teacher told us about a contest to design the logo for the football team. I loved horses and was always sketching them. My love for reading stories of the West and watching cowboy movies led me to the name Mustang. I thought it was a cool name and submitted it along with a sketch of a horse. I won the contest, one of the only contests I ever won in my life. I was very pleased and proud to see that name and logo applied to the team.

Q: Is this the Penn Yan mustang as you drew it? Or has it been tweaked over the years?
A: No, I believe my sketch was in the same vein as that, but my horse was running. Pretty much the same horse in a different pose. I think it looks great though. Whoever "tweaked" it did a very good job. I like it as well or better than mine (as I remember it).

The present-day Penn Yan Mustang. *Public domain.*

Q: Did you develop your interest in guitar during those years?
A: Yes. I had been playing a few chords on guitar that my father taught me when I was almost six years old. My aunt had sent me a lap steel [Hawaiian] guitar and I actually took two or three lessons on it from a guy named Tracy Calkins [Cawkins?] there in Penn Yan. But I preferred the guitar, and for some reason, lessons on the guitar were not available at the time. Mr. Calkins liked my steel playing, however, and invited me to play with him on his fifteen-minute radio show he did on Saturday afternoons in Hornell, New York. We played "Missouri Waltz," and that was the first time I played an instrumental on radio.

Q: I met a man who remembered you playing and singing at the Grange Hall in Guyanoga. Did you play there? Where else in the area?
A: I did play at the Grange Hall. It was directly opposite our store. As I recall, I played and my sister sang a couple of songs. I also played and sang a couple of songs for an assembly during the eighth grade in Penn Yan Academy. I did a Hank Williams song, "Long Gone Lonesome Blues," and a Stuart Hamblin song, "It Is No Secret." I got through both without a mishap, and the audience seemed to like my performance. I was twelve at the time.

Q: Why did your family leave the area?
A: My father said he was tired of the cold winters and shoveling snow. He wanted to go somewhere warmer. It was a toss-up between Florida and Arizona. I campaigned for Arizona, as I wanted to see real cowboys and Indians. I guess he and my mother liked the idea of going west, so that's where we went.

Q: What else do you remember about your time in Yates County?
A: I remember the summers with great fondness. There was a sort of summer camp down on the shore of Lake Keuka just east of Branchport. They had all kinds of activities for kids of all ages, including swimming classes. As you know, those spring-fed Finger Lakes are cold! But when you are a kid, you get used to it quickly. I still remember floating in that cool water and looking at the blue sky and the surrounding hills. It was an idyllic and a beautiful place to be as a child.

I also remember that when my parents sold the store, my father wasn't ready to set out across the country yet. He always aspired to be a writer and was working on a novel. He rented a farmhouse in the little crossroads of Yatesville, and we spent most of the summer there while he wrote. My cousins came to visit and my sister, little brother and I had a wonderful summer playing in the old barn and around the countryside. Then, in August, we set out to drive to Tucson, Arizona, where I began my teenage years and grew up to become a musician.

Duane Eddy through the years: (left to right) 1948, 1958, 2012. *Photos courtesy of Duane Eddy.*

The building that once housed the Eddy store in Guyanoga is long gone. The Grange Hall, which is the old Larzalere Tavern, is now a private residence. Duane Eddy left Yates County to go on to a highly successful career that had a very real impact on the music industry. According to one biography, "In the early days of Rock and Roll, the notion of the lead guitarist as the charismatic figure in the spotlight was completely novel. Duane Eddy moved the guitar player front and center. Quiet and unassuming offstage, he cut an indelible figure with an electric guitar in his hands. It was a classic pose that defined the cool iconography of what it means to be a Rock and Roller."[13] He has produced over thirty albums, the most recent in 2011. His twangy guitar can be heard as part of the soundtracks for movies including *Forrest Gump*, *Natural Born Killers* and *Broken Arrow*. He has received accolades from his peers, including a Grammy in 1986 for the Best Rock Instrumental ("Peter Gunn"). He was inducted into the Rock and Roll Hall of Fame in 1994 and the Musician's Hall of Fame in 2008, and he was the recipient of *Guitar Player Magazine*'s Legend Award in 2004.

A big thank-you goes to Duane Eddy for providing this interview. If you have never heard him play his "twangy guitar," just plug his name into YouTube and play "Rebel Rouser" and a few other numbers. His official website is www.duane-eddy.com.

22
THE LAST MAN AT THE BENHAM

As the country was drifting toward civil war in 1860, a new state-of-the-art hotel was under construction on Main Street in Penn Yan. The major downtown hotel up to that time, the American Hotel (located where Long's Bookstore is today), burned down in 1857, leaving the village without a first-rate hotel. Editor Stafford C. Cleveland of the *Yates County Chronicle* complained on March 1, 1860: "For weeks when strangers arrive in town, the only public places they can find to shelter them from the storm are the awnings and sheds in front of the stores. Now after a lapse of two years we are nearly as destitute as ever. An appeal to public minded citizens follows asking them to contribute so that the stigma which now rests on Penn Yan may be removed."

A number of Penn Yan businessmen answered the call and raised part of the money needed for construction of a new hotel, and the rest was put up by DeWitt Benham, the son of the first sheriff of Yates County. Ground was broken on Main Street in August 1860, and the hotel opened for business in October of the following year under the name the Benham House. The *Yates County Chronicle* at the time described it as "a large, commodious and elegant building." For almost one hundred years, the hotel changed ownership and management many times, but it remained the finest hotel in Penn Yan. The building was kept up to date with upgrades to heating, lighting and plumbing. The four-story hotel had fifty guest rooms, which were described as light, airy and well furnished. The main floor had a dining room, which could seat 125 people and was known for its excellent food. The dining room was

The Benham Hotel on Main Street in Penn Yan, circa 1950s. *Courtesy of YCHC.*

the scene of numerous wedding celebrations, private parties and banquets, as well as a meeting place for community organizations. The hotel was the place to put up VIPs visiting Yates County, including Theodore Roosevelt and various congressmen. Franklin and Eleanor Roosevelt both spoke there.

By the 1950s, the building, although well maintained over the years by its various owners, was starting to show its age. The last owners, Mr. and Mrs. Harvey Hirsch, sold the building in 1959 to the Lincoln Rochester Trust Company, which made plans to raze the old hotel and build a new bank building on the site (now the Community Bank). The owners, who had an apartment in the hotel, notified all residents that the contents of the building would be auctioned off in April 1959 and the building demolished in August. Refusing to believe the notice was eighty-nine-year-old Allie Lackey, who made no plans to vacate his room. Lackey was a retired printer from Rochester who had retired to Dundee. After breaking a hip and being hospitalized for three months, he moved into the Benham Hotel early in 1958. As the time approached for the auction of the contents of the hotel fourteen months later, the owners started to put pressure on Lackey to leave. They refused to take the harsh measures of cutting off his heat, lights and delivered meals. Instead, they raised his rent to ten dollars a day. He refused

HAVE BED, WON'T TRAVEL — Auctioneer Victor Pirrung, left, sold the bed on which he is seated for $25 at the auction at the Benham Hotel in Penn Yan Friday, but Allie Lackey, the stubborn 89-year-old retired printer, refused to leave. The buyer will wait.

Going, Going, Gone! All but Allie and Bed

Left: Clipping from the *Rochester Democrat and Chronicle* from April 1959. *Courtesy of YCHC.*

Below: The Benham Hotel being razed in 1959. YCHC collection. *Courtesy of YCHC.*

to pay. They then ordered the hotel handyman to cut off delivery of cigars to Lackey's room. He had a three-cigar-a-day habit, and they hoped that this would force him out of his room in order to go out and buy some. Then the owners could lock the doors. That didn't work either. Finally, the owners took legal measures and served him with an eviction notice. He replied by saying if they want him in court, they would have to hold it in his room.

In late April 1959, the auction was held at the Benham Hotel. When the auctioneer got to the contents of Allie Lackey's room, the bed had to be auctioned off with Lackey still in it. The man, who paid twenty-five dollars for the bed and other contents of the room, said that he was willing to wait until Lackey was out of it before picking up his purchase. That didn't happen right away, as Lackey held out in his room. Sympathetic people continued to supply him with food and cigars. As the date for razing the building approached and before force had to be used to remove him, Allie Lackey left the Benham Hotel on his own volition and was soon situated in a local nursing home. He died there in November 1960 at the age of ninety.

The destruction of the Benham Hotel in August and September 1959 provided some insight for those interested in mid-nineteenth-century architecture and construction techniques. Frank Swann, Yates County historian at the time, wrote this for the September 17, 1959 *Chronicle-Express*:

> *Several curious old time methods of construction have been disclosed by Joe D'amico and his wreckers as the old Benham House is practically down to bare earth. Over the dining room, supporting the ceiling and upper floors were two arched beams of cast iron, perhaps 28 feet long. These were brittle and broke easily as the contractor's bulldozer dragged them from the building. In fact, one beam was already broken and in a few years would unquestionably have caused real trouble. These arched beams weighed about 1,500 pounds each and were possibly the product of the old Commercial Iron Works then located not far away. Heavy wooden timbers about 8 by 12 inches supported the beams, that suggested modern steel I-beams. Ornamental caps over many of the windows that appeared to be of plaster actually were cast iron. Several of them have already been sold to local persons who propose to make pairs of Benham bookends.*

Others in the community bought batches of brick, stone and other salvaged articles. Thus, the Benham, along with Allie Lackey, became part of our county history.

This story was inspired by Penn Yan resident and Yates County History Center member Dick Eisenhart, who did a program at a history luncheon for us in May 2010. Dick spent many years as the local reporter for the Rochester *Democrat and Chronicle*. Among the many entertaining stories that he told at the luncheon was the story of Allie Lackey. I talked to Dick about the story afterward, and he gave me the clippings from his 1959 articles on the topic. They are now on file in the Research Room at the Underwood Museum.

NOTES

Part I

1. Kolmerten, "Ernestine L. Rose."
2. Stanton, Anthony, Gage and Harper, *History of Woman Suffrage*.
3. *Yates County Chronicle*, April 5, 1922.
4. Adams, 1977 summer supplement.
5. Ibid.
6. *Chronicle-Express*, January 9, 1936.

Part II

7. *New York Times*, November 22, 1916 (from Old Fulton Postcards).
8. *Chronicle-Express* Bicentennial Edition, July 1976.

Part III

9. Reprinted in an unidentified local newspaper clipping from August 1930 found in the "Albertson" family file at the Yates County History Center.
10. Cleveland, *History of Yates County*, 1:715.

11. Interview of unnamed "elderly Penn Yan resident" conducted by Penn Yan resident Paul Birmingham in 2004. The interview is in the YCHC files.
12. Assumption College's E Pluribus Unum Project, http://www1.assumption.edu/ahc.

Part IV

13. Biography provided by Duane Eddy.

BIBLIOGRAPHY

Adams, William. The 1977 summer supplement of the *Chronicle-Express*.

Cleveland, Stafford C. *History of Yates County, New York*. Vol. 1. Penn Yan, NY: Yates County Chronicle, 1873.

Harvey, Steven. *It Started with a Steamboat: An American Saga*. Bloomington, IN: Authorhouse, 2007.

Klees, Emerson. *Paul Garrett: Dean of American Winemakers*. Rochester, NY: Friends of the Finger Lakes Publishing, 2010.

Kolmerten, Carol. "Ernestine L. Rose: Free Thinking Rebel." *Free Inquiry* 22, no. 3 (n.d.)

Philbrick, Nathaniel. *In the Heart of the Sea: The Tragedy of the Whaleship* Essex. New York, NY: Penguin Books, 2000.

Local Newspapers

Chronicle-Express

Corning Evening Leader

Dundee Observer

Yates County Chronicle

Yates County Whig

Internet Resources

New York Times Article Archives. www.nytimes.com.

Northern Illinois University Libraries, Beadle and Adams Dime Novel Digitalization Project. http://www.ulib.niu.edu/badndp/bibindex.html.

Old Fulton Postcards. www.fultonhistory.com/Fulton.html.

Raul Literature Weblog. http://literature6r.wordpress.com/assignment-2-moby-dick.

Stanton, Elizabeth Cady, Susan B. Anthony, Matilda Joslyn Gage and Ida Husted Harper. *History of Woman Suffrage*. Vol. 1. Project Gutenburg, n.d. http://www.gutenberg.org/ebooks/28020.

Yesterday's Papers, a blog written by Canadian John Adcock. http://john-adcock.blogspot.ca/2011/08/leon-lewis-1833-1920.html.

ABOUT THE AUTHOR

Courtesy of Charles R. Mitchell.

Rich MacAlpine was born in Geneva, New York, but was raised in New Jersey. He graduated from Transylvania University in Lexington, Kentucky, and did graduate work at Colgate University in Hamilton, New York. For thirty-four years, Rich taught European and American history at Oneida High School in Oneida, New York. During that time, he developed an interest in researching family history, which started his relationship with the Yates County History Center in Penn Yan, New York. After retiring from teaching in 2001, he and his wife, Jeanie, moved to a home on Keuka Lake just outside Penn Yan, where he became more than just a researcher in the history center. He has served on its board of directors since 2006 and has served as editor of its bimonthly publication, *Yates Past*, since 2008. The MacAlpines have three adult children and nine grandchildren.